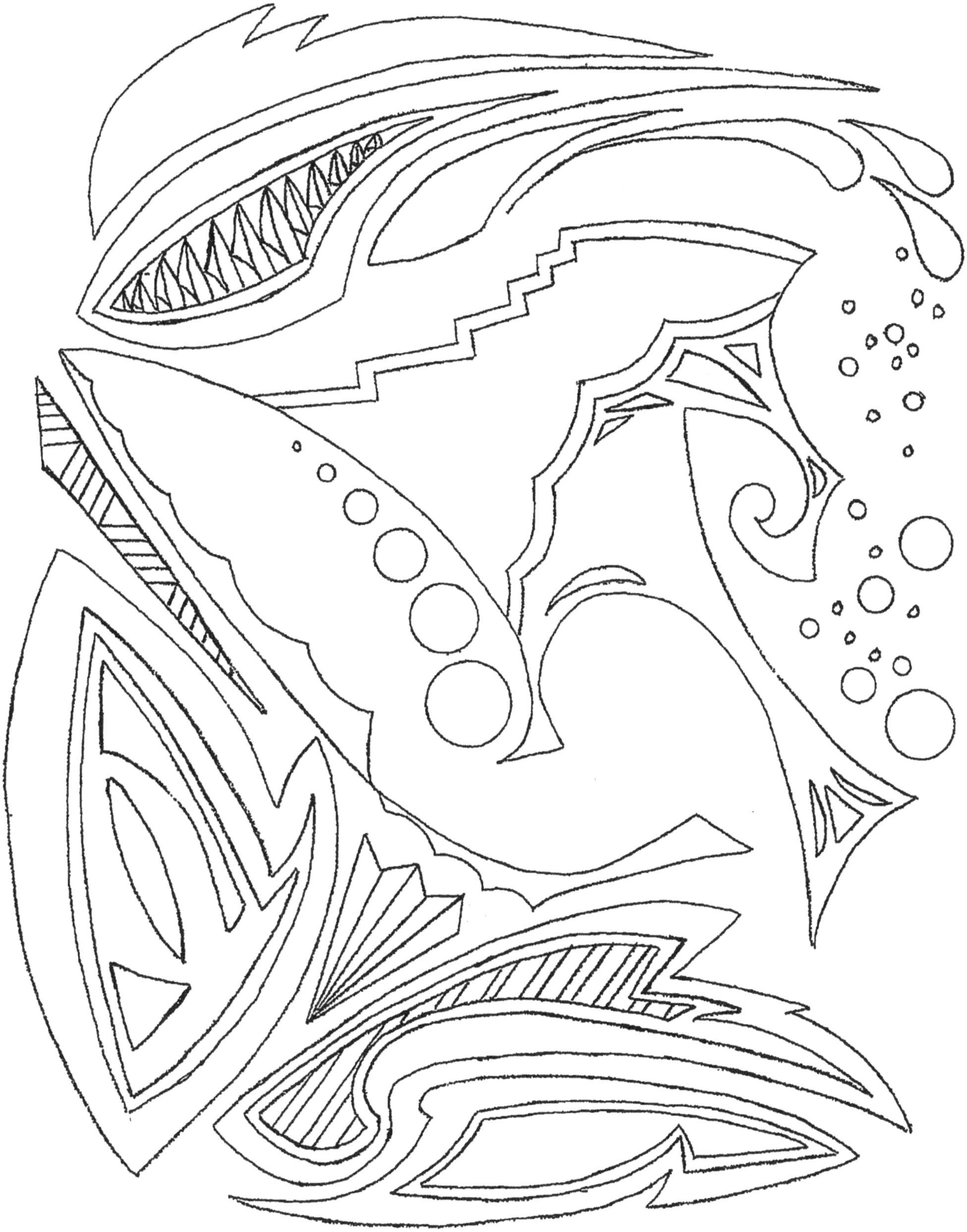

KISS: Keep It Simple, Stupid

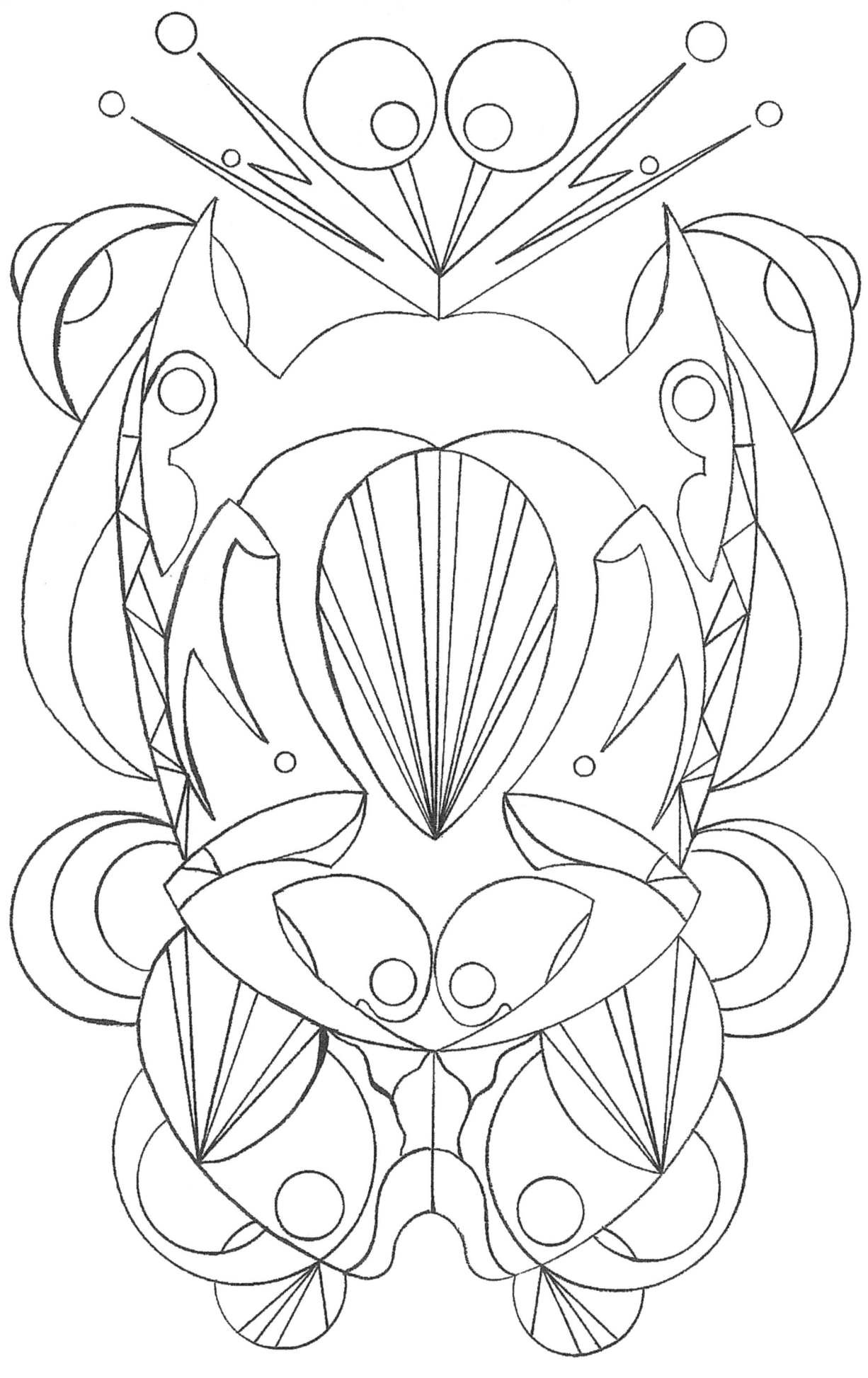

SLIP: Sobriety Losing Its Priority

SLIP: Sobriety Losing Its Priority

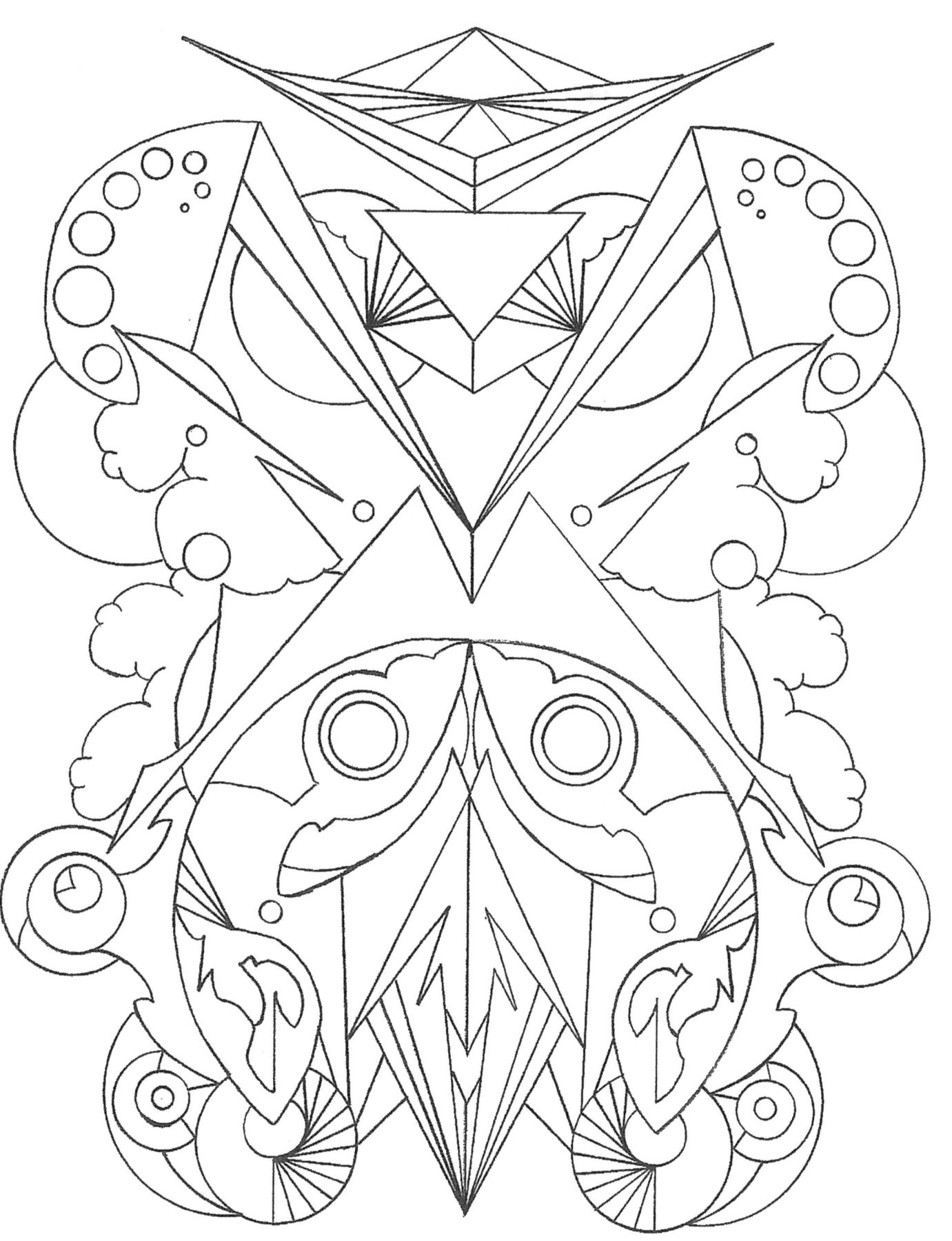

Let Go and Let God

Let Go and Let God

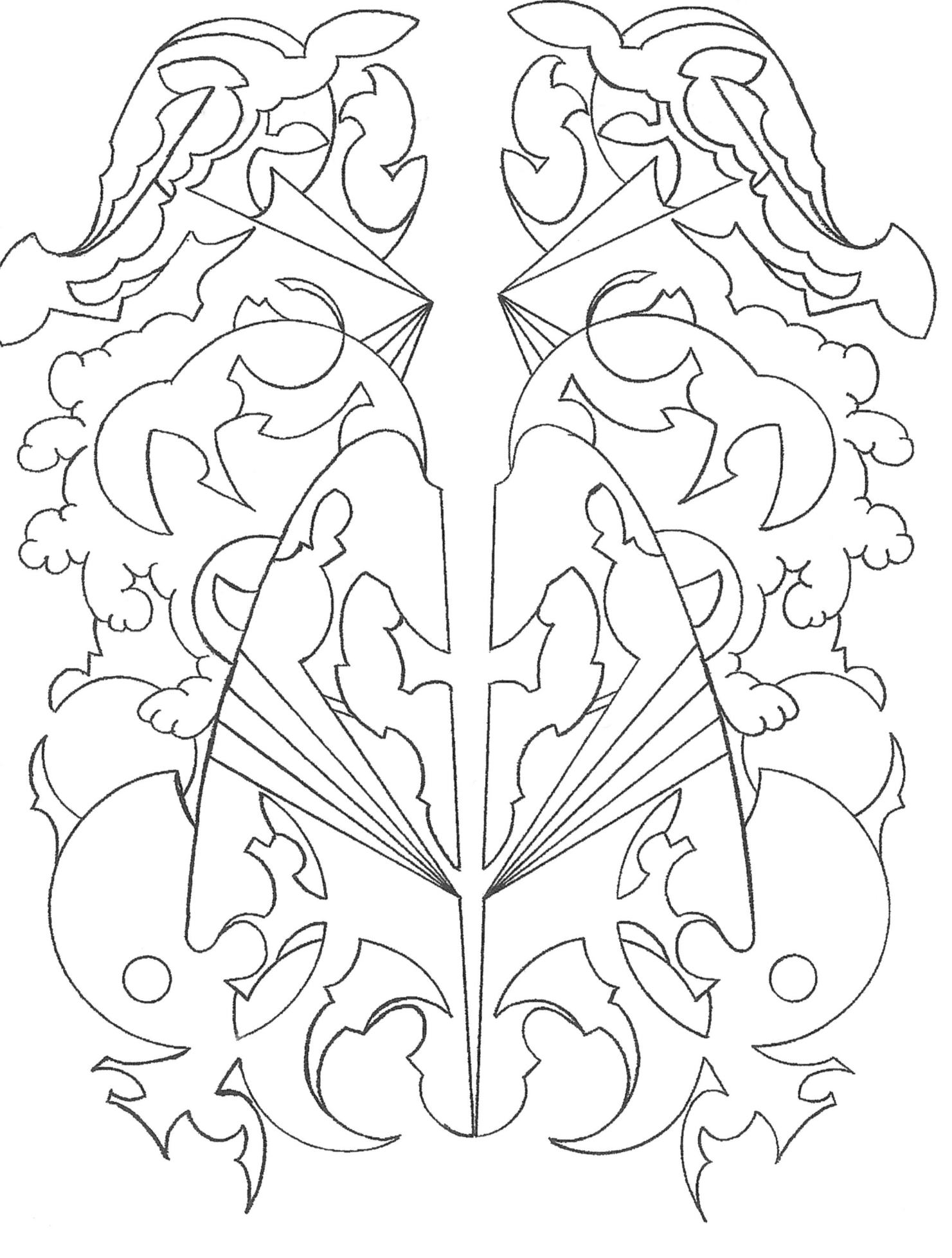

Under every dress there's a slip.

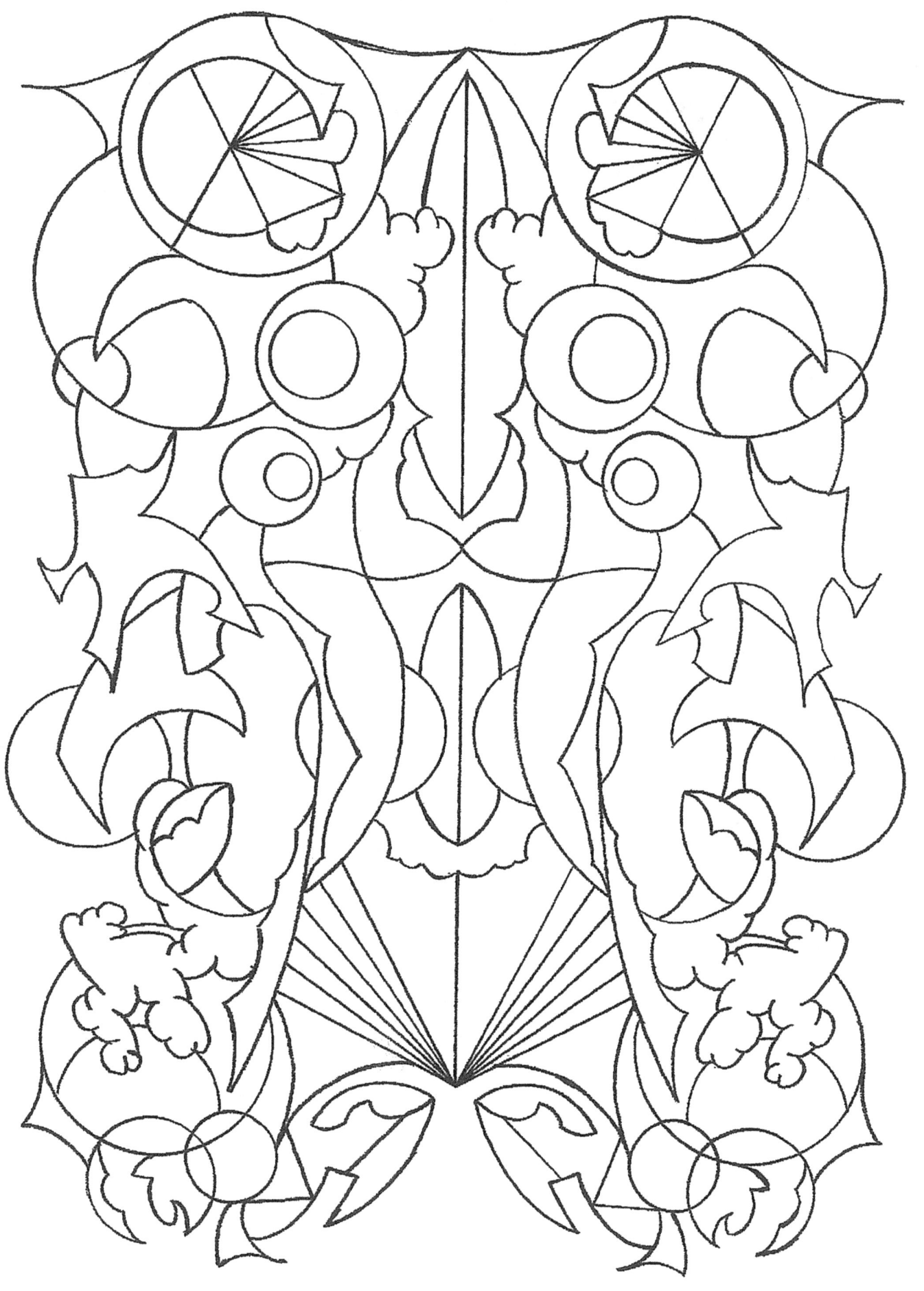

I've been here a few 24 hours.

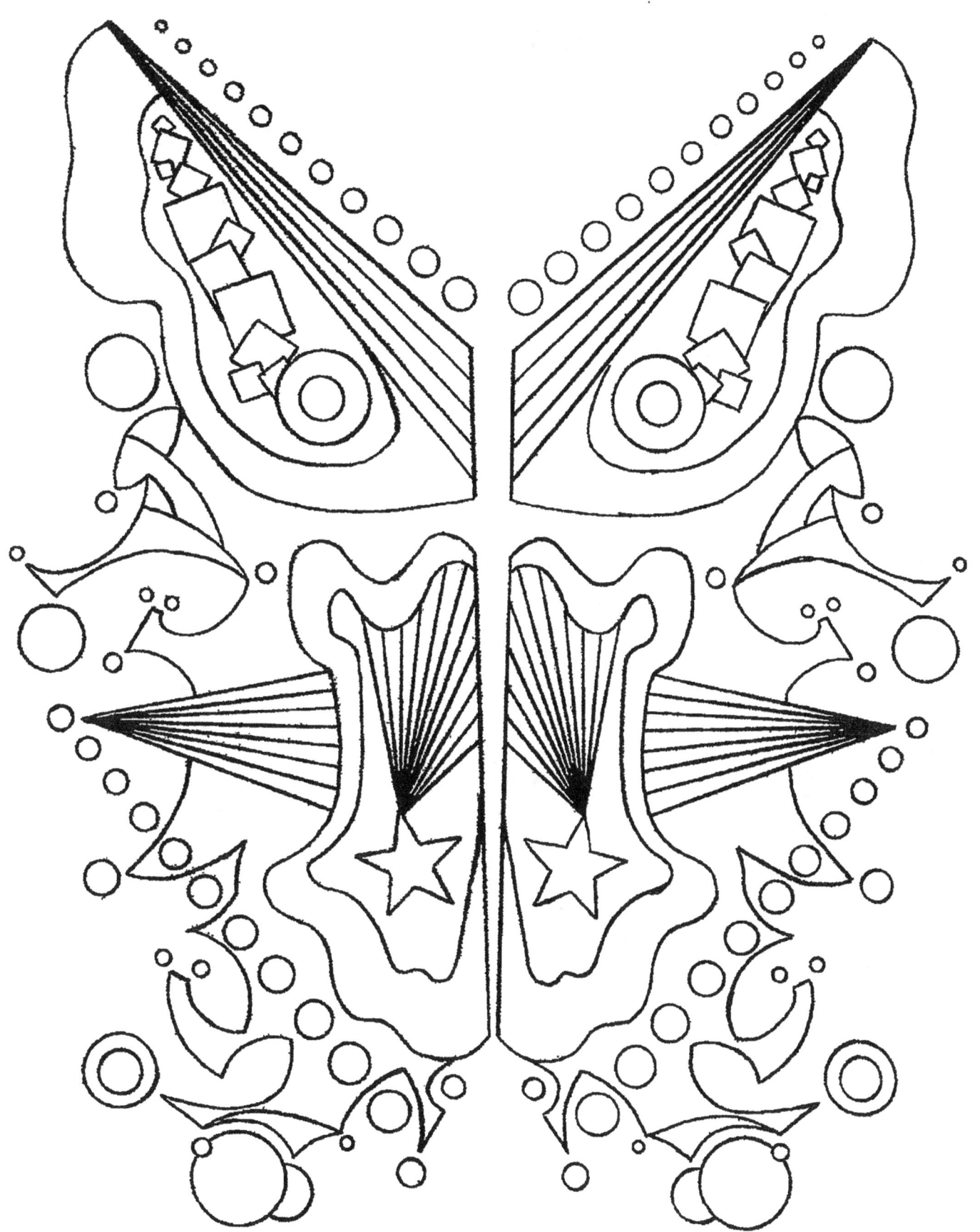

Just For Today

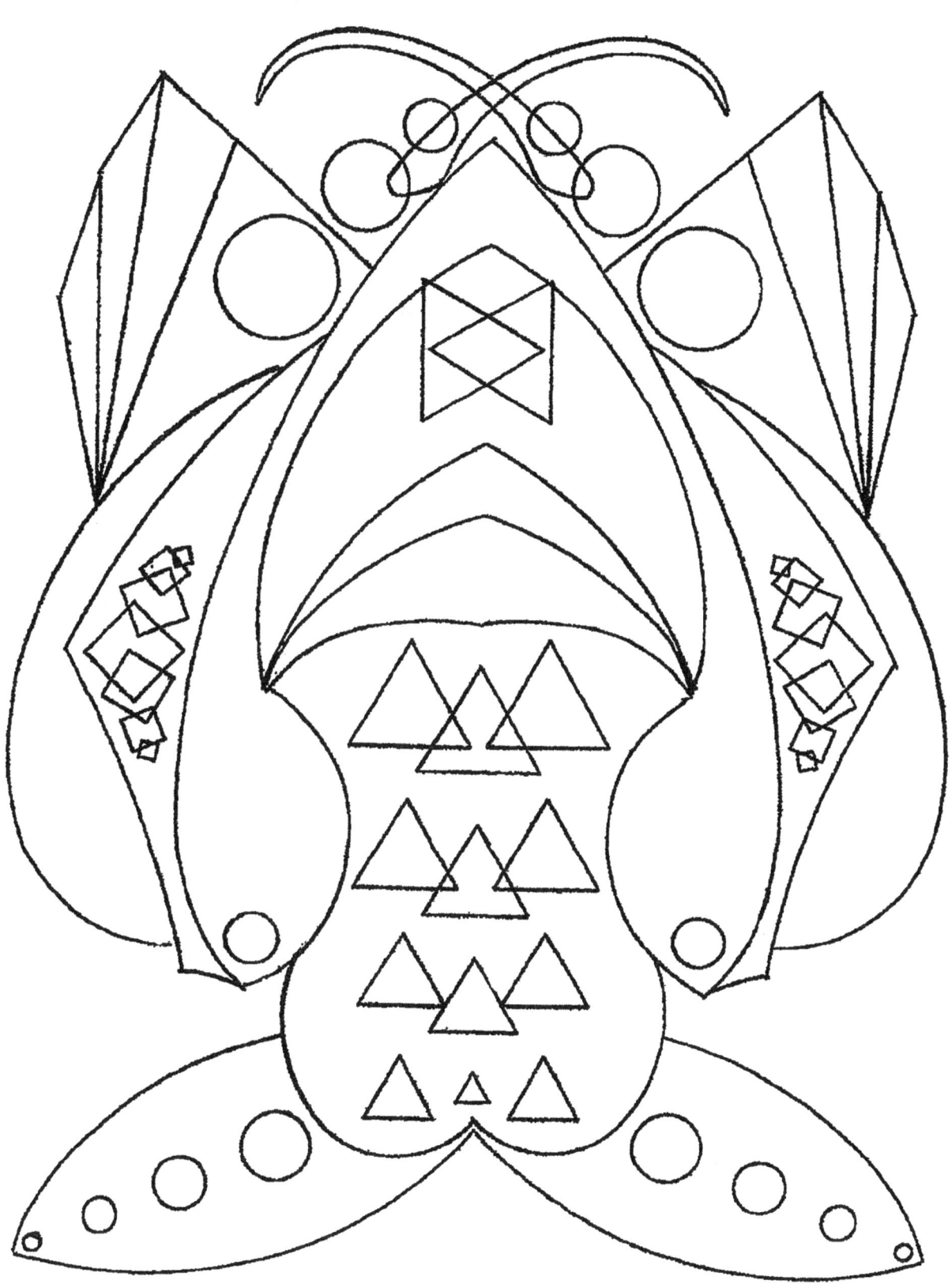

Keep coming back.

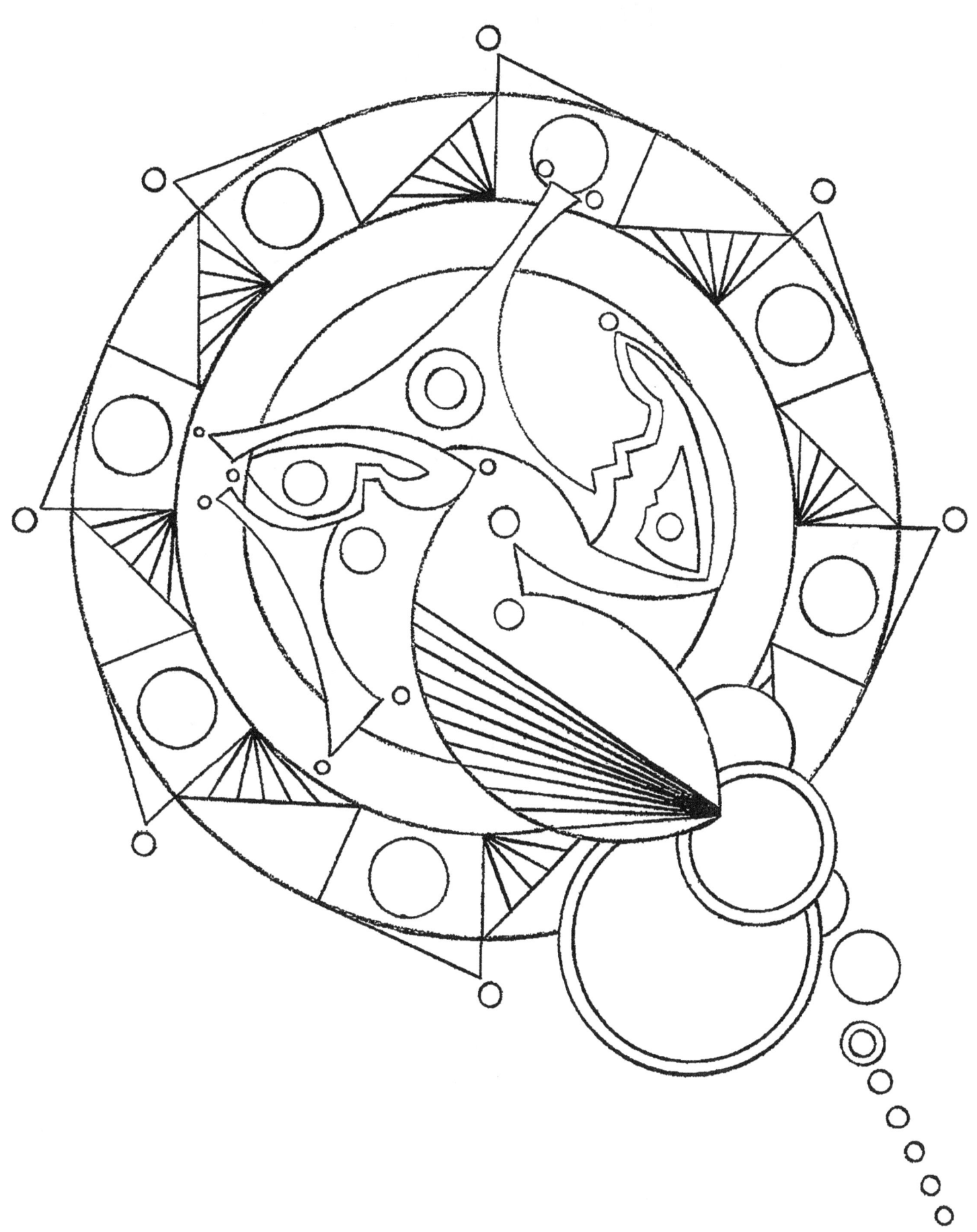

Stick with the winners.

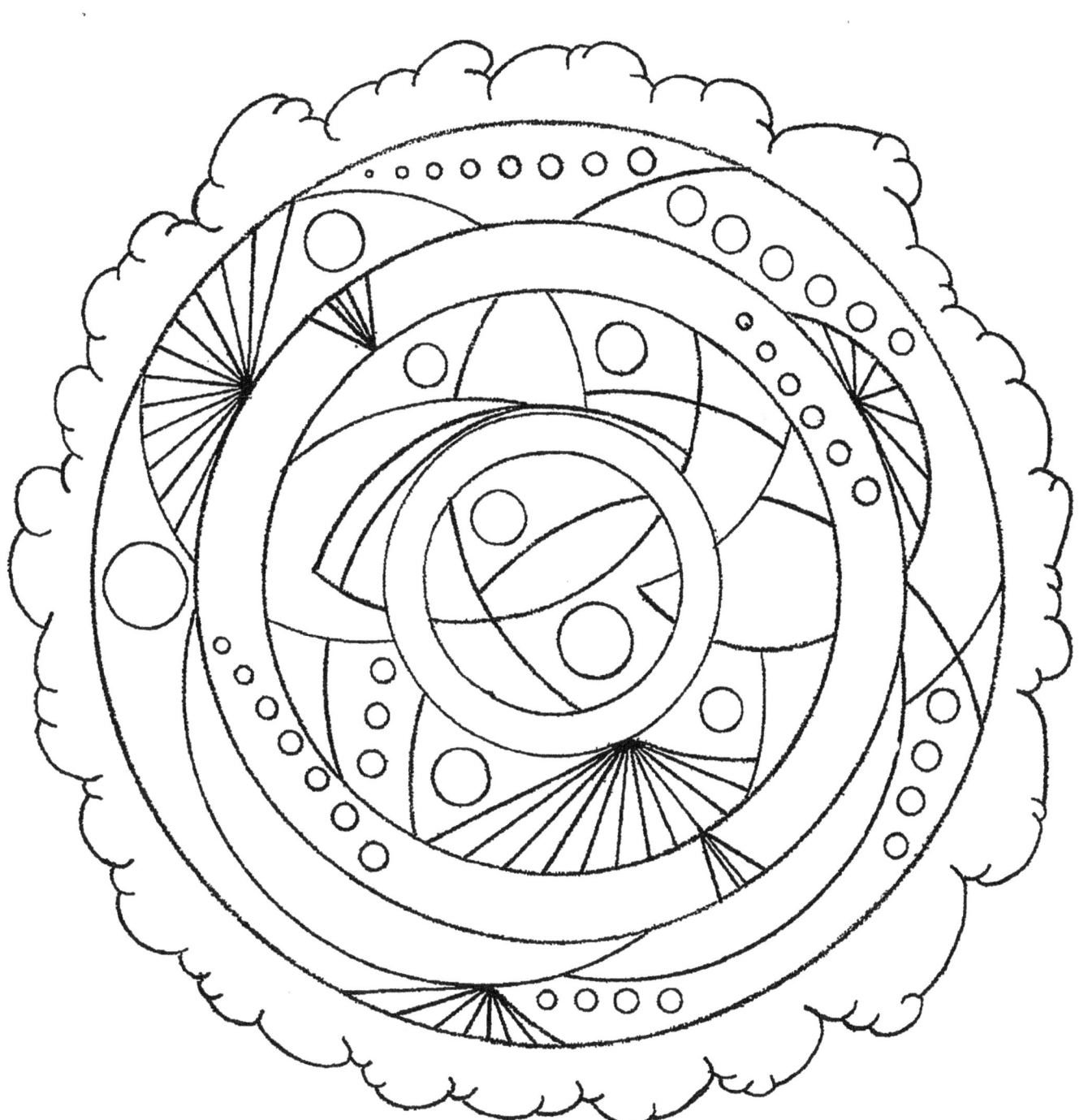

It's a selfish program.

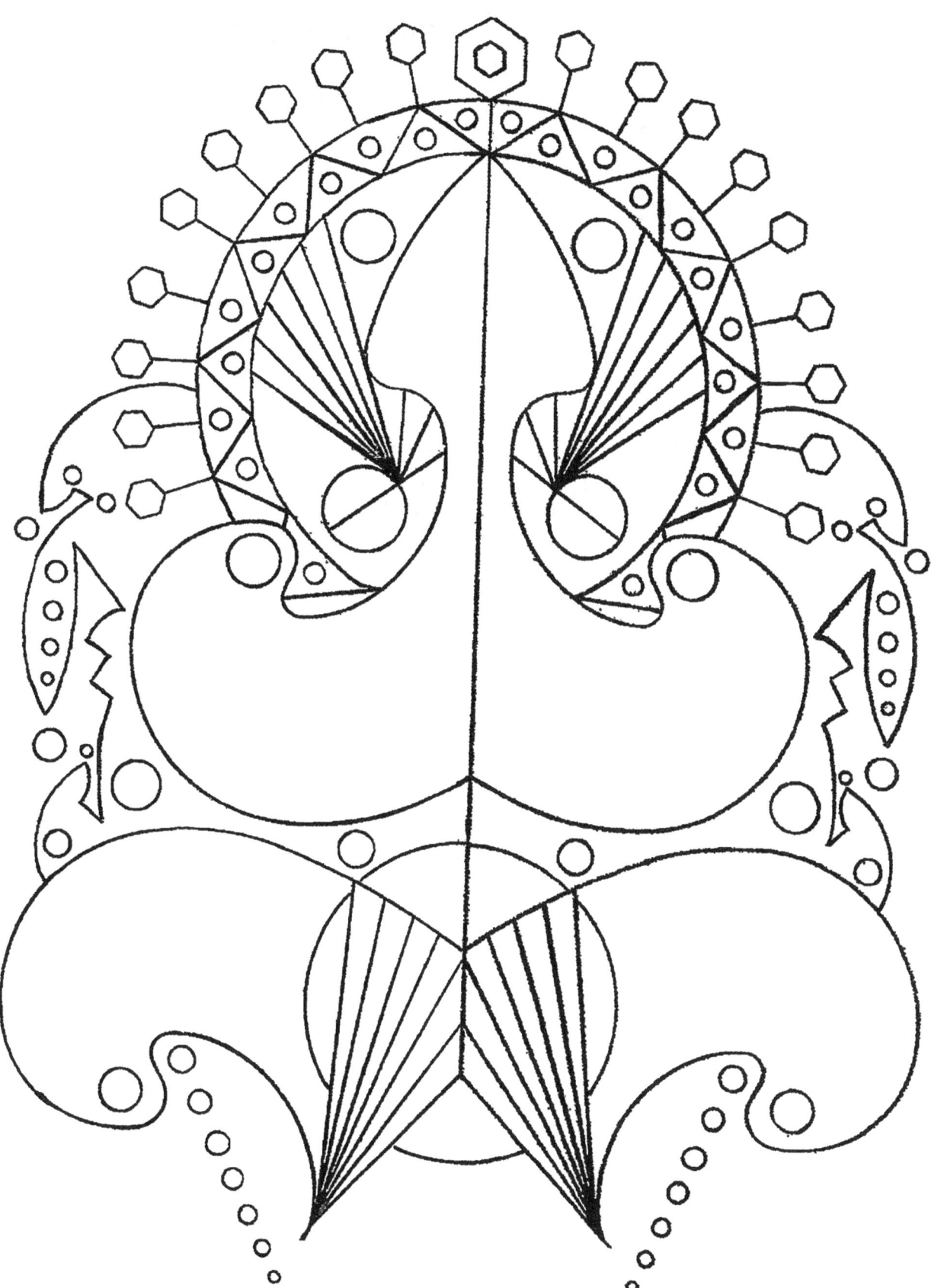

Fake it till you make it.

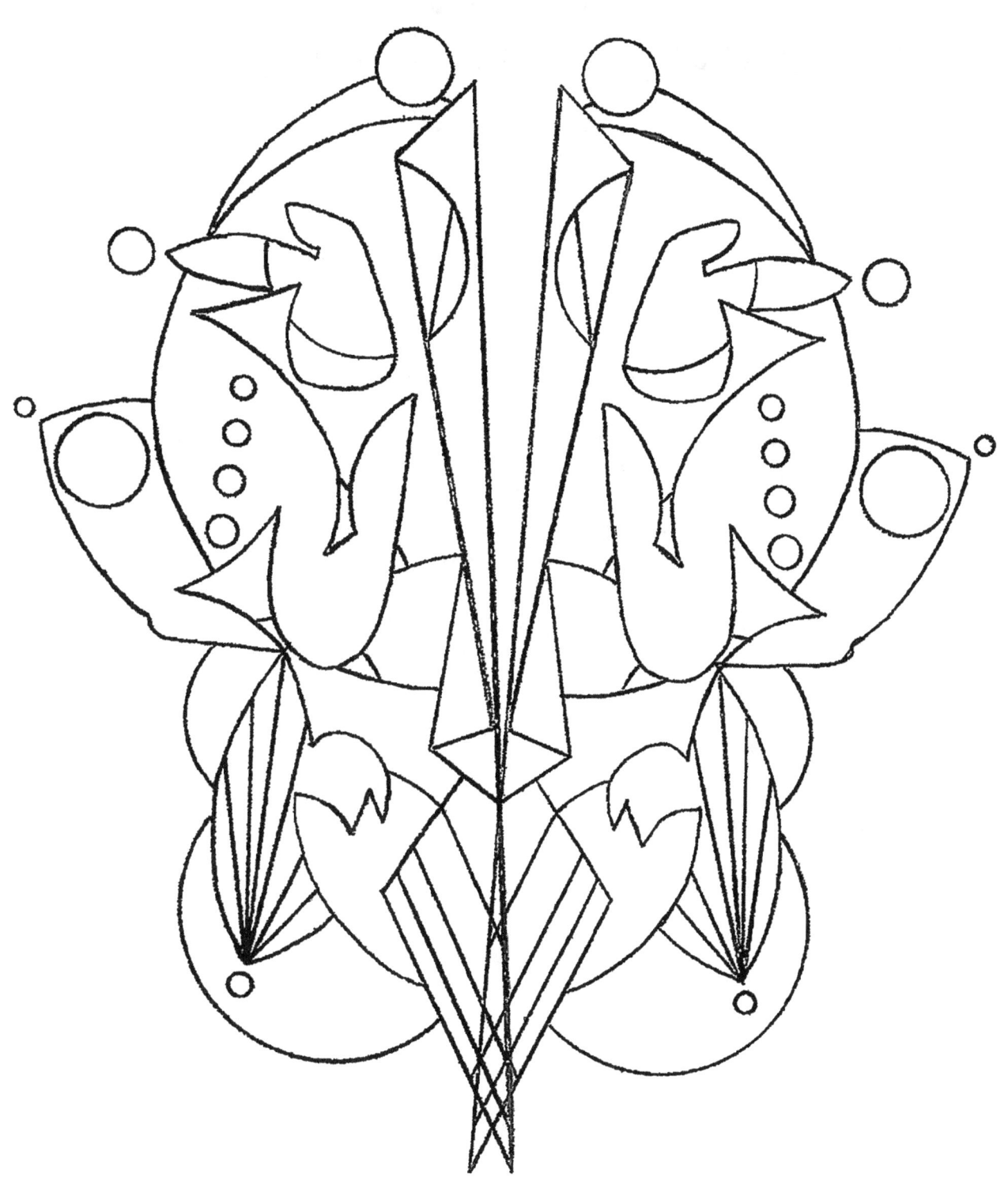

Don't try to recruit people before they're ready --
they'll have you drinking before you'll get them sober!

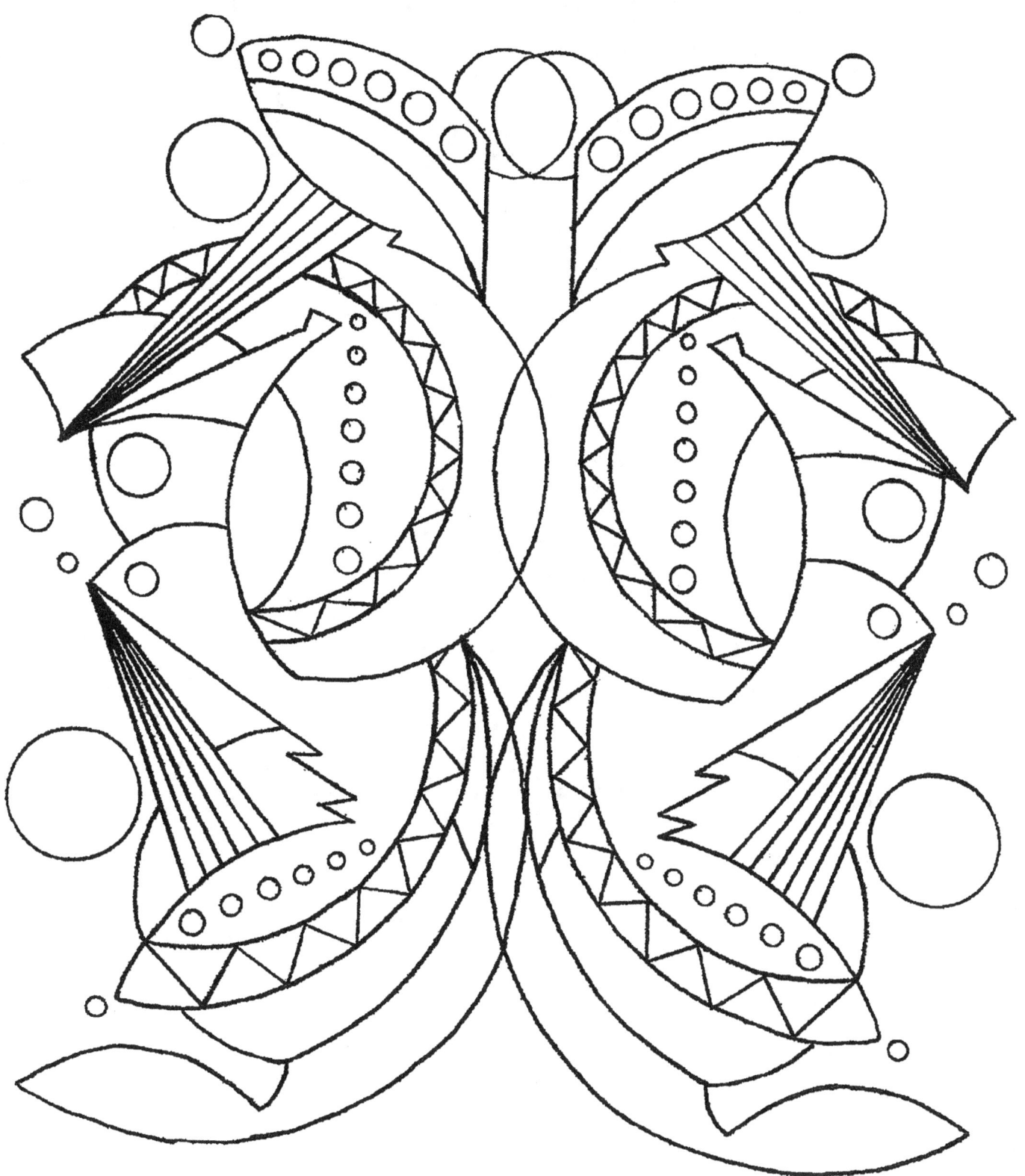

Poor me, poor me, pour me a drink.

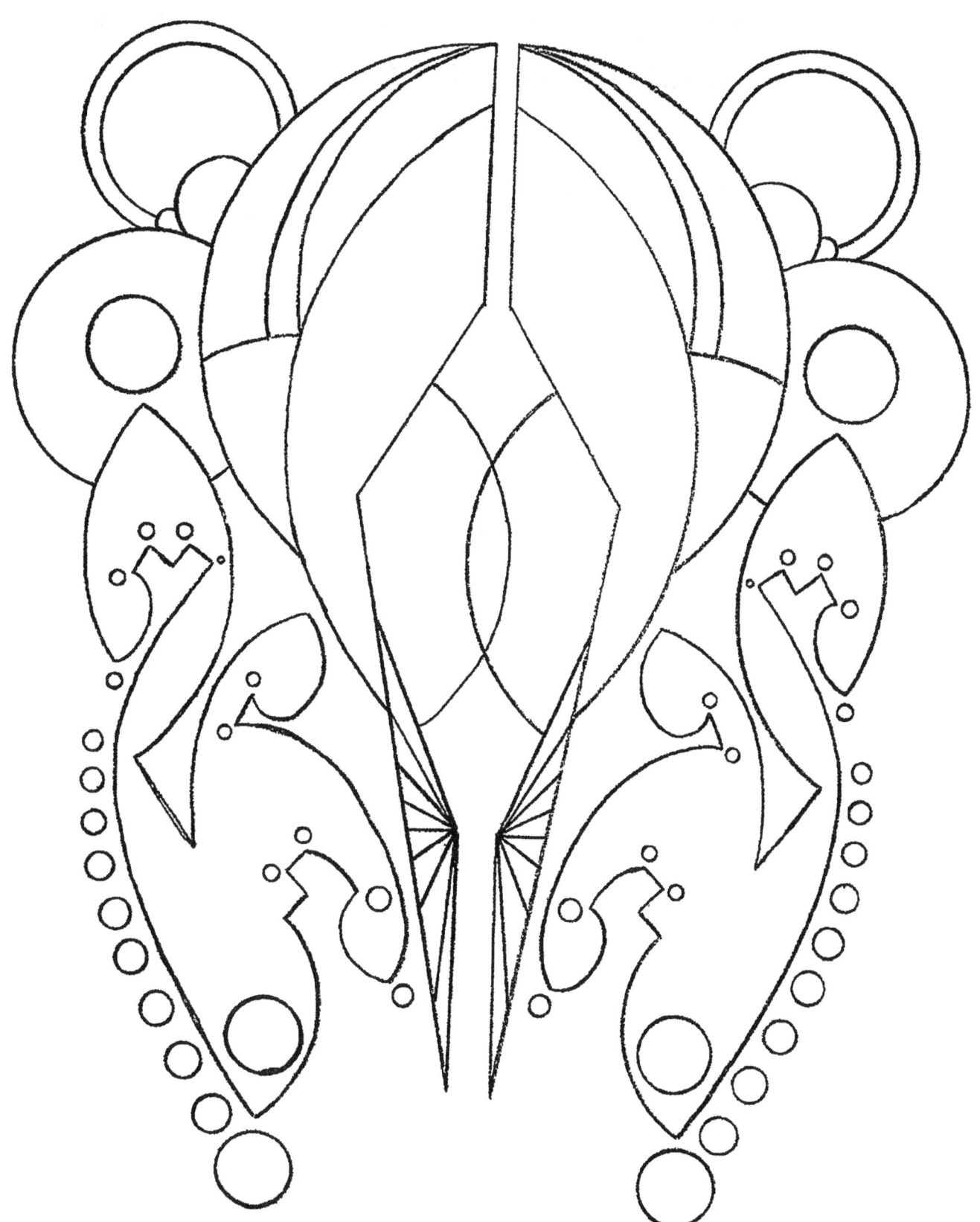

If you hang around a barber shop long enough, you'll get a haircut.

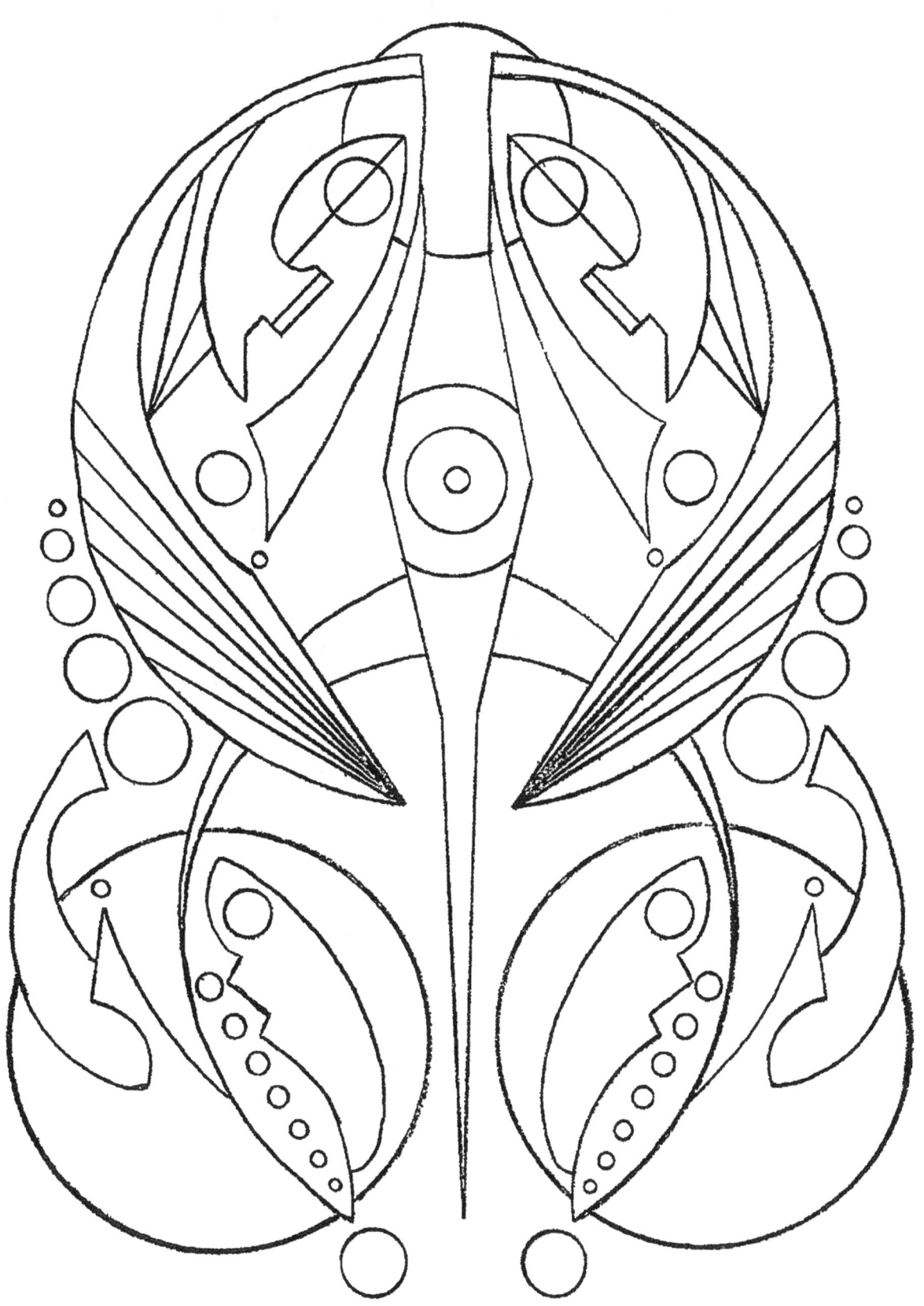

You have to give it away in order to keep it.

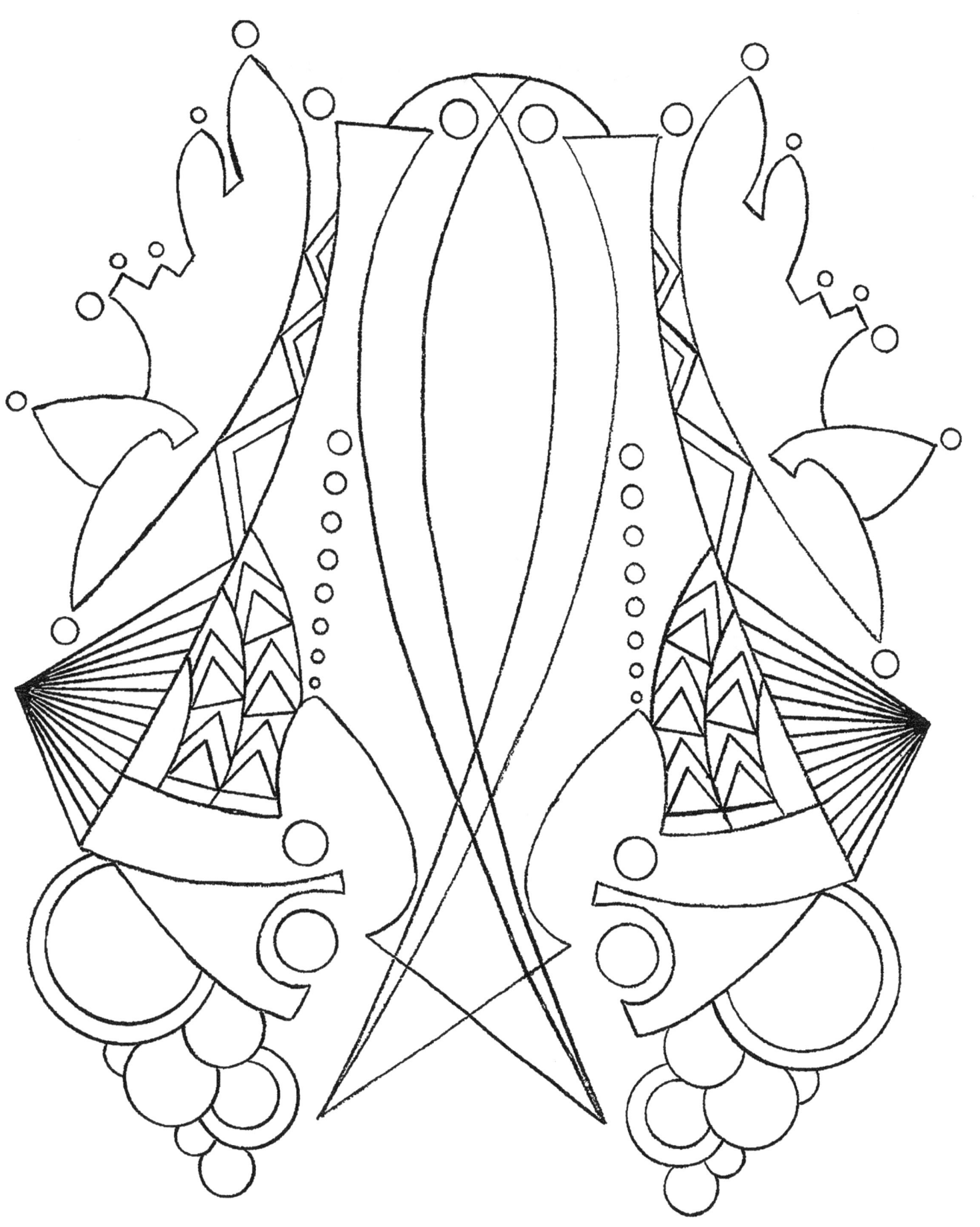

Gratitude is an attitude.

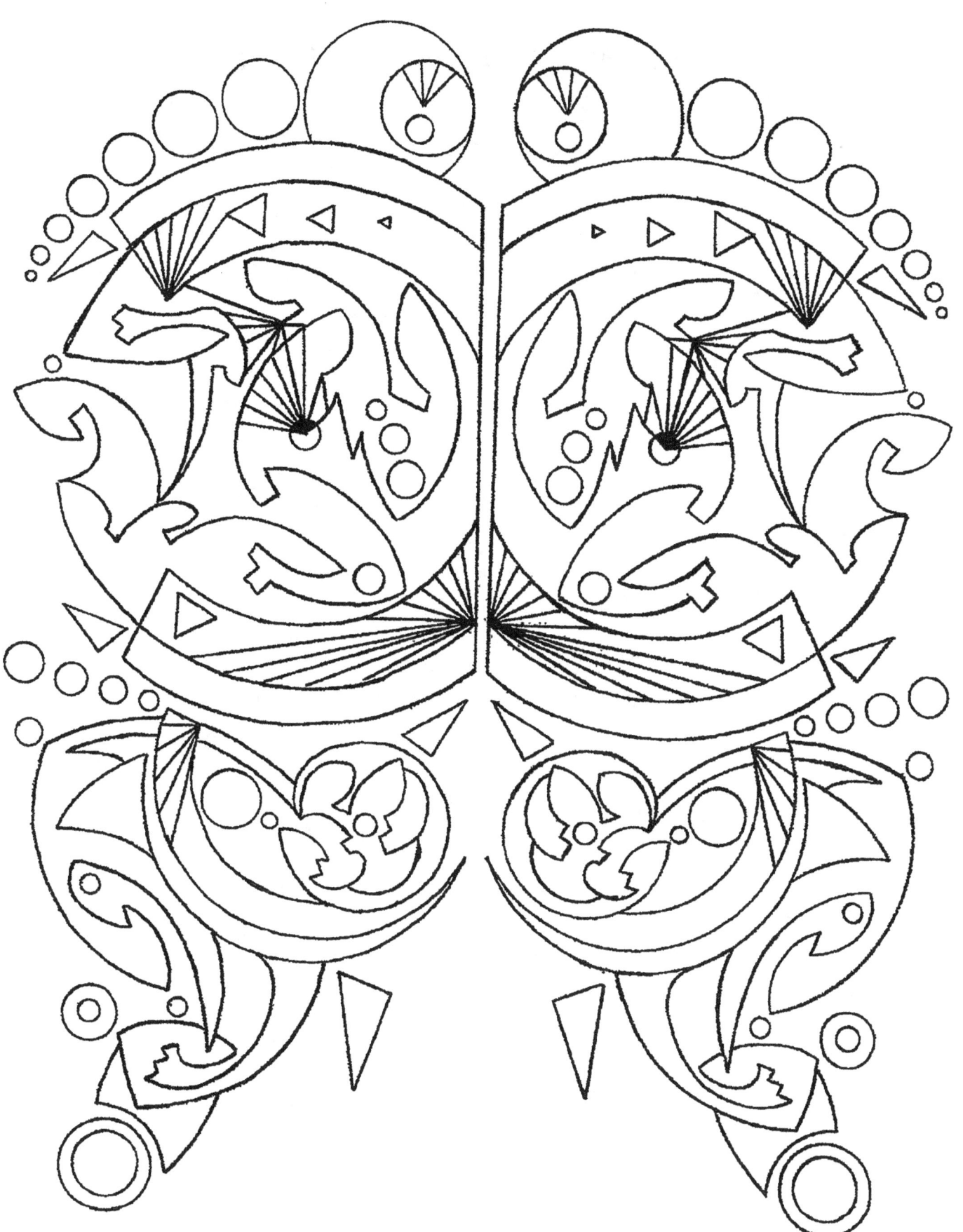

Get an attitude of gratitude.

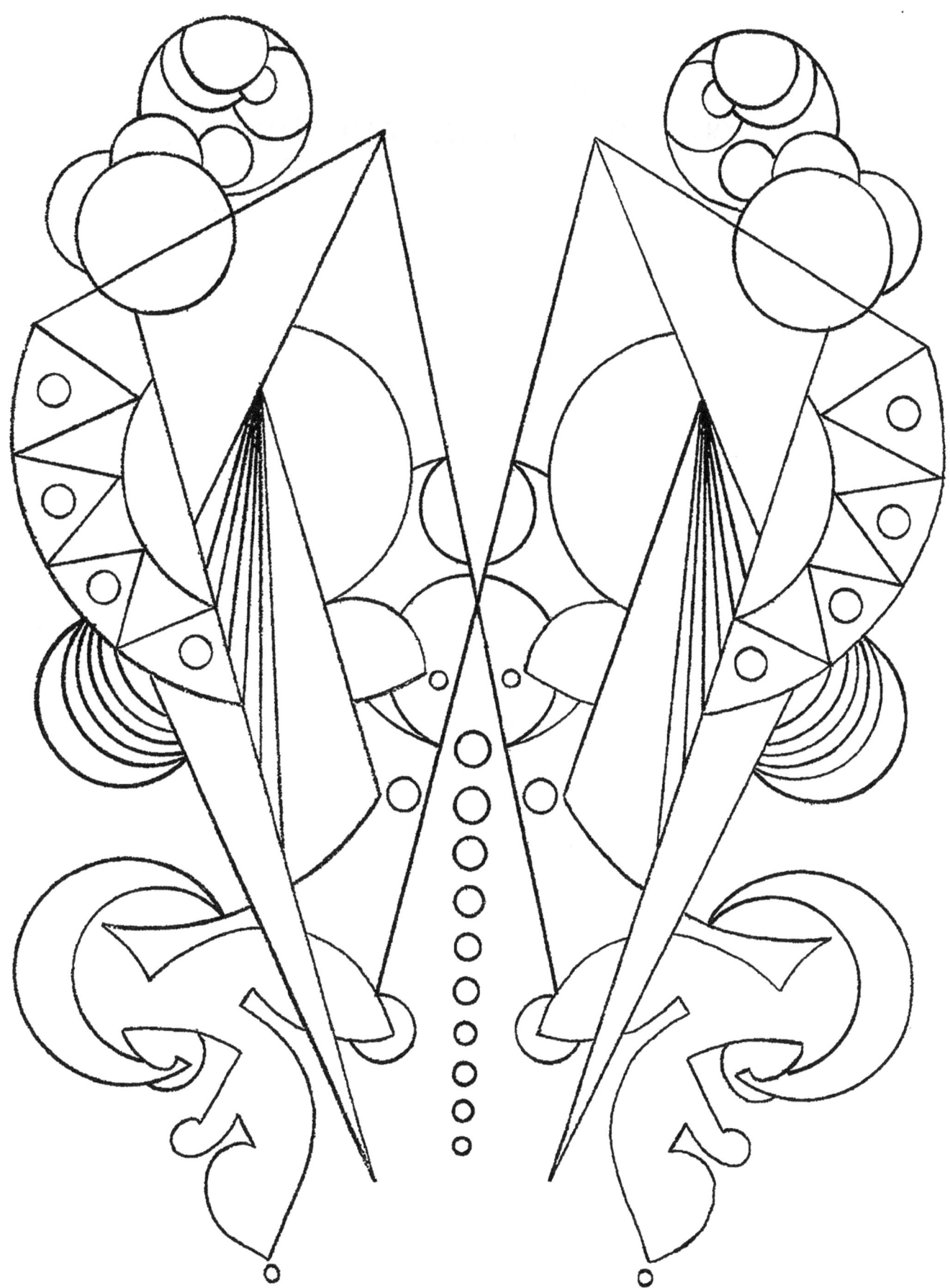

It's easy to talk the talk,
but you have to walk the walk.

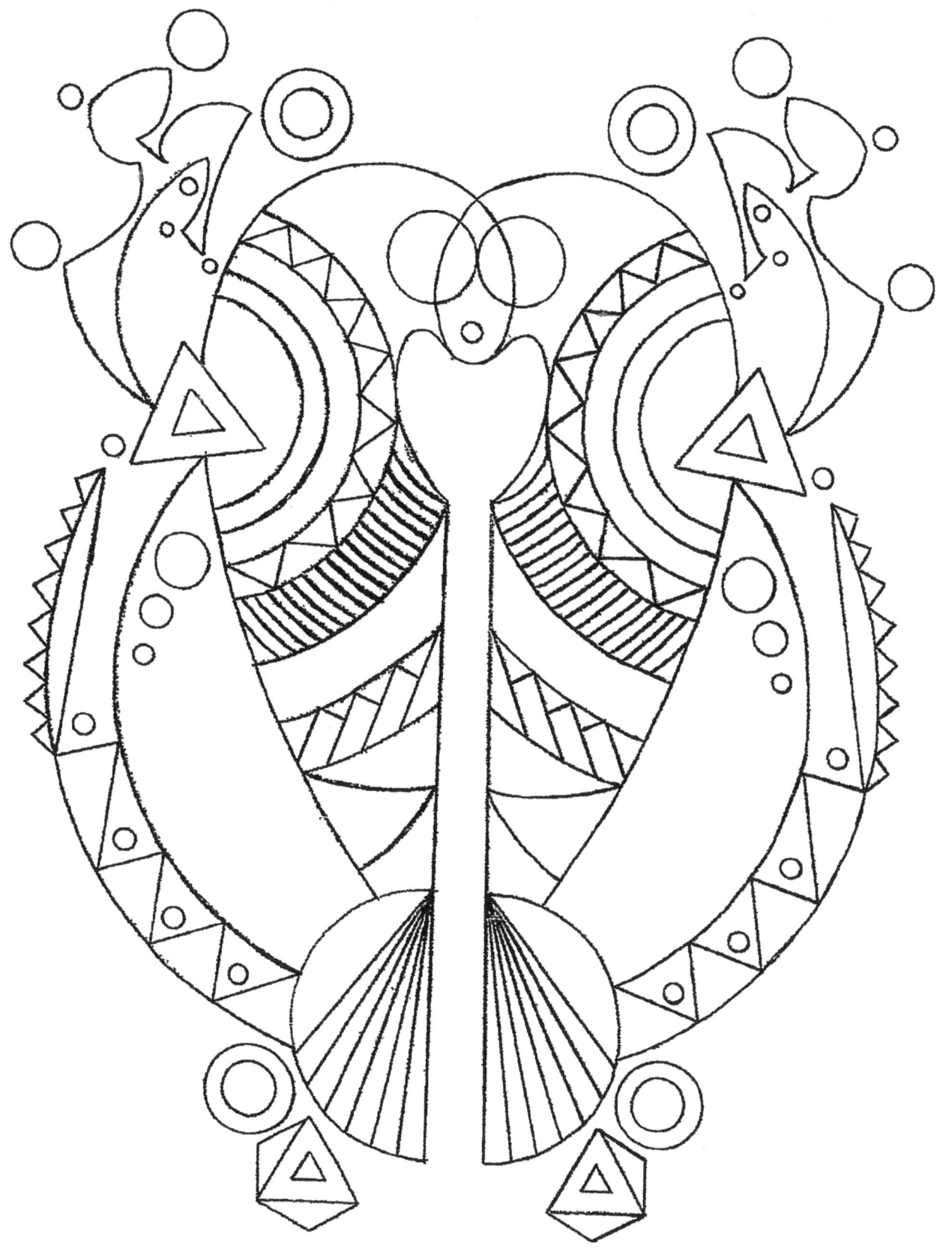

I got sick and tired of being sick and tired.

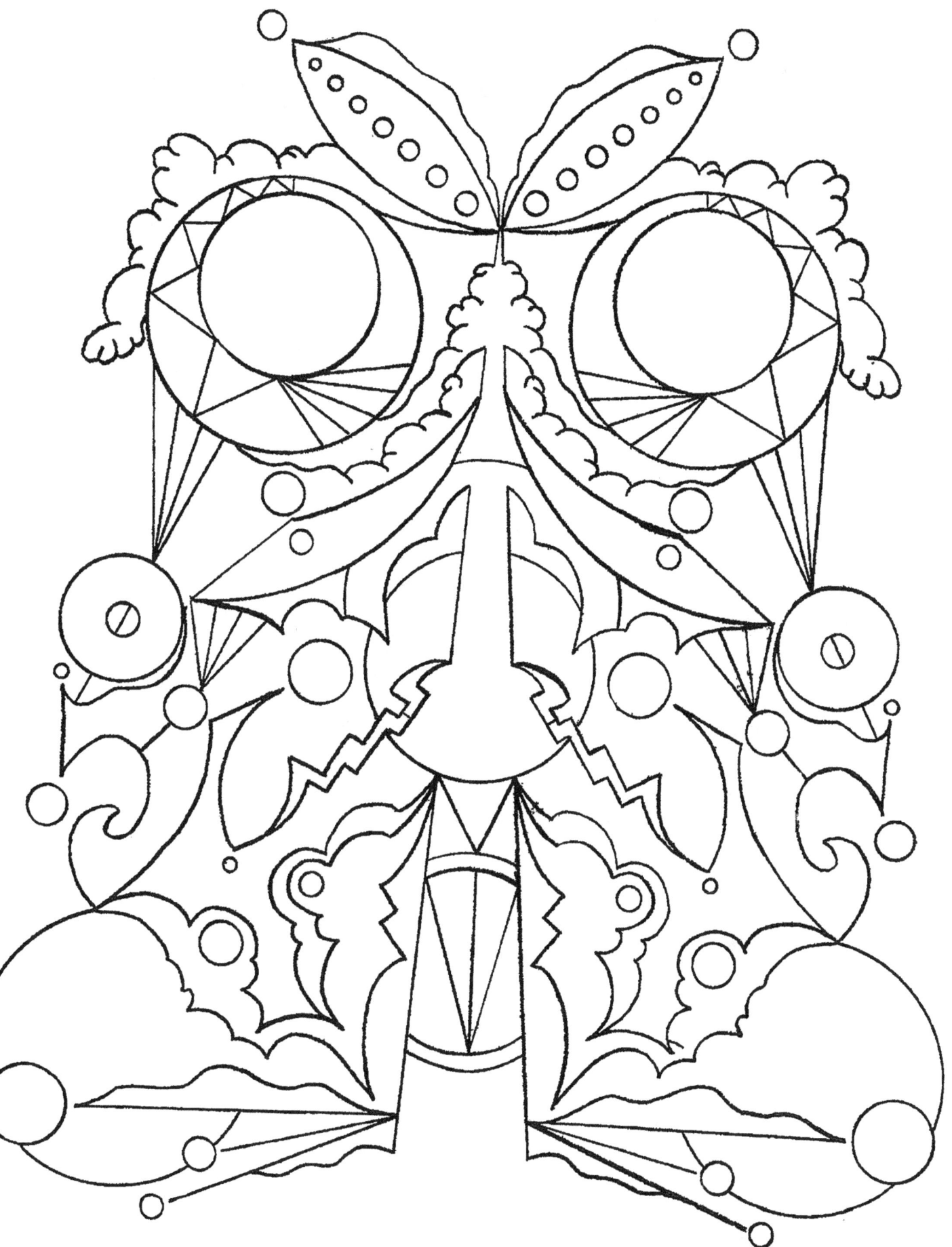

If you fly with crows, you'll get shot at

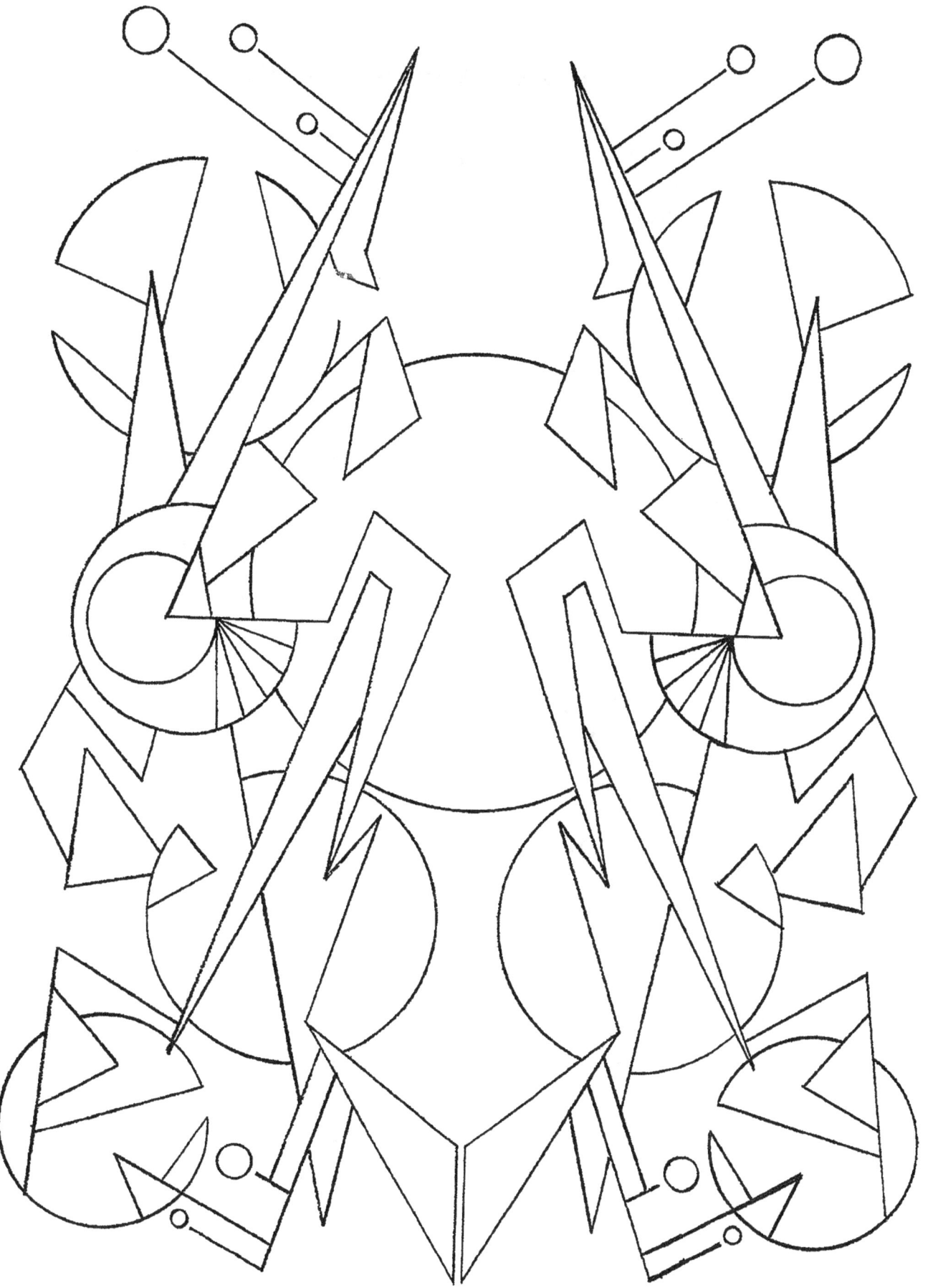

One Day at A Time

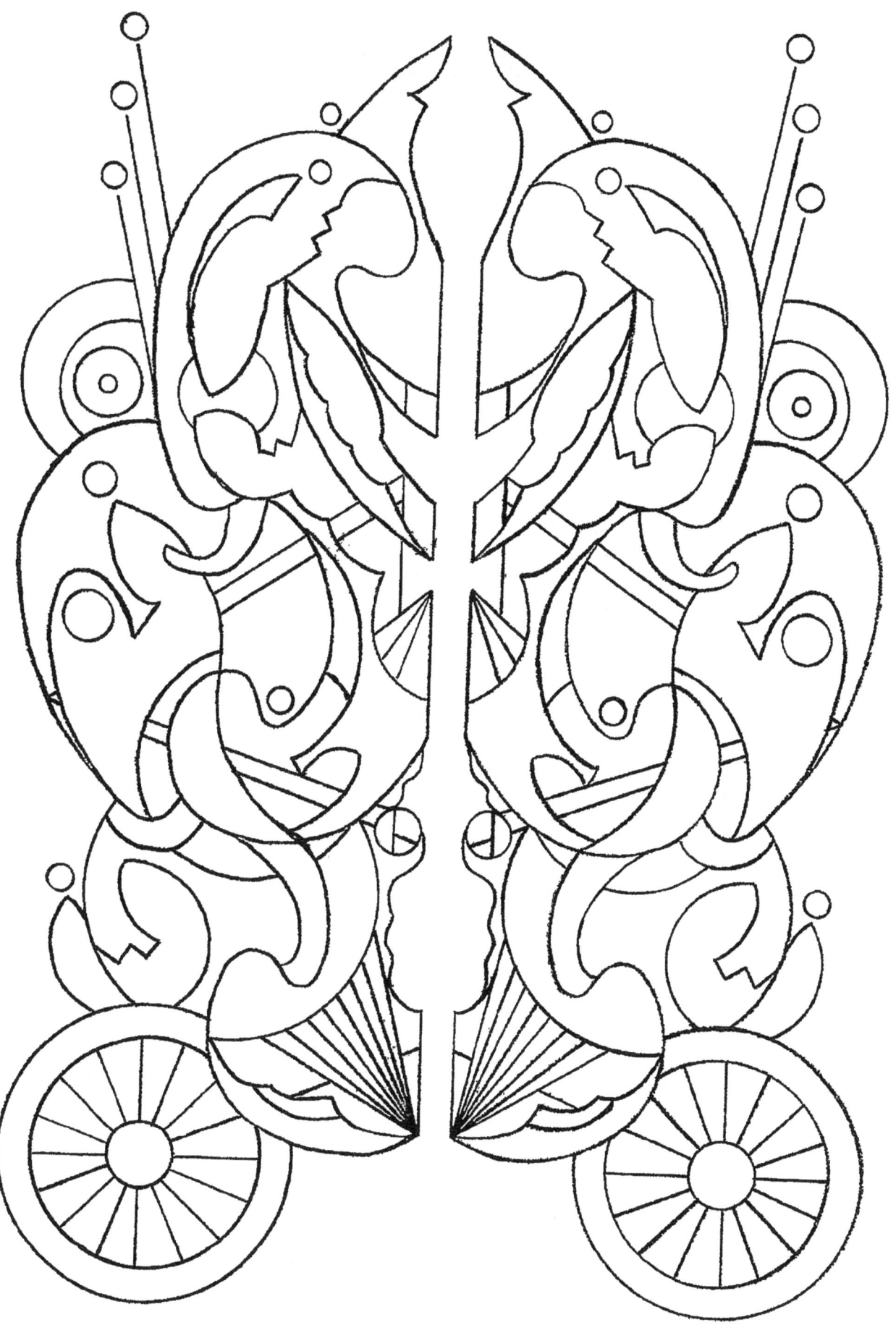

Easy Does It

Easy Does It

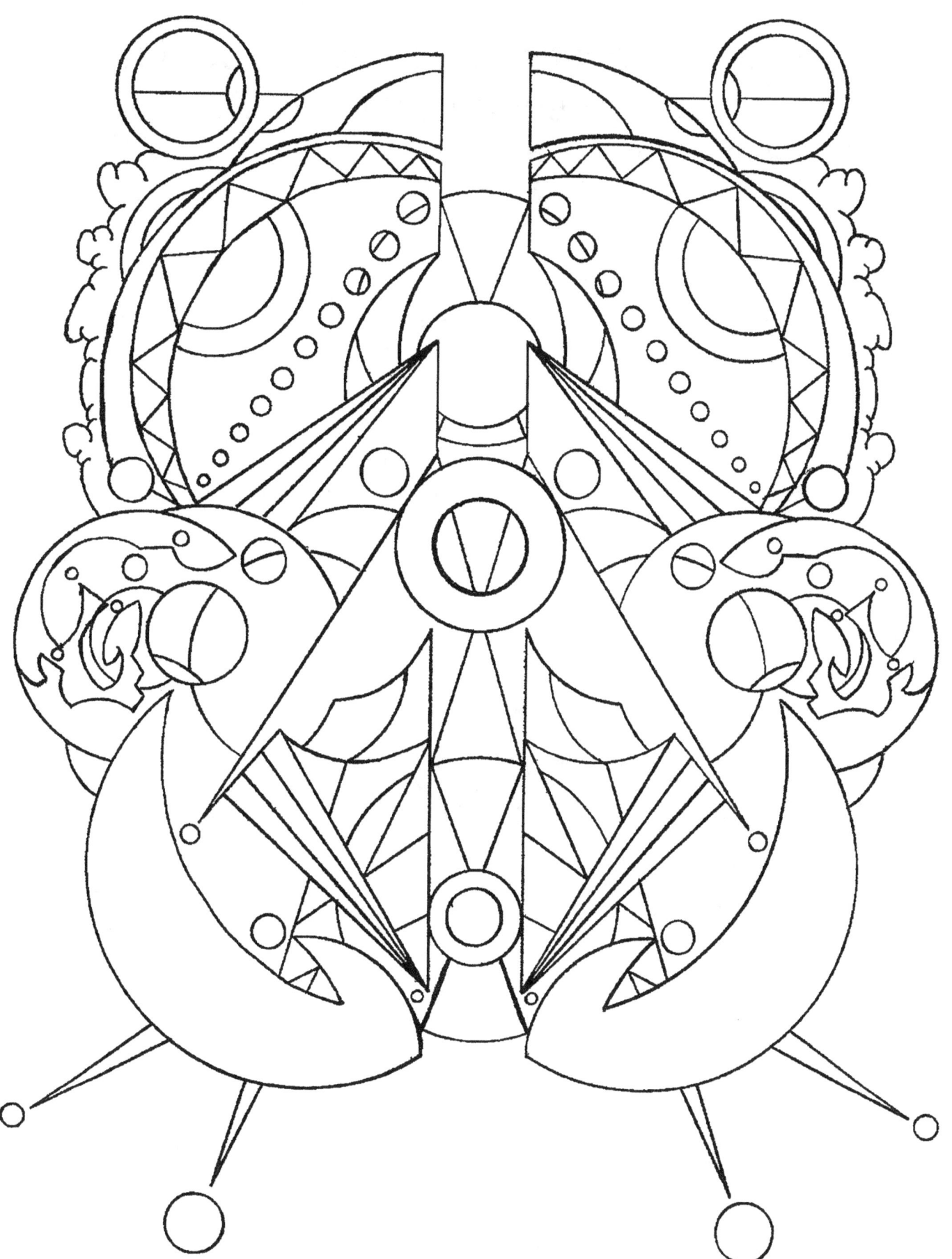

If drinking doesn't bring you to your knees, sobriety will.

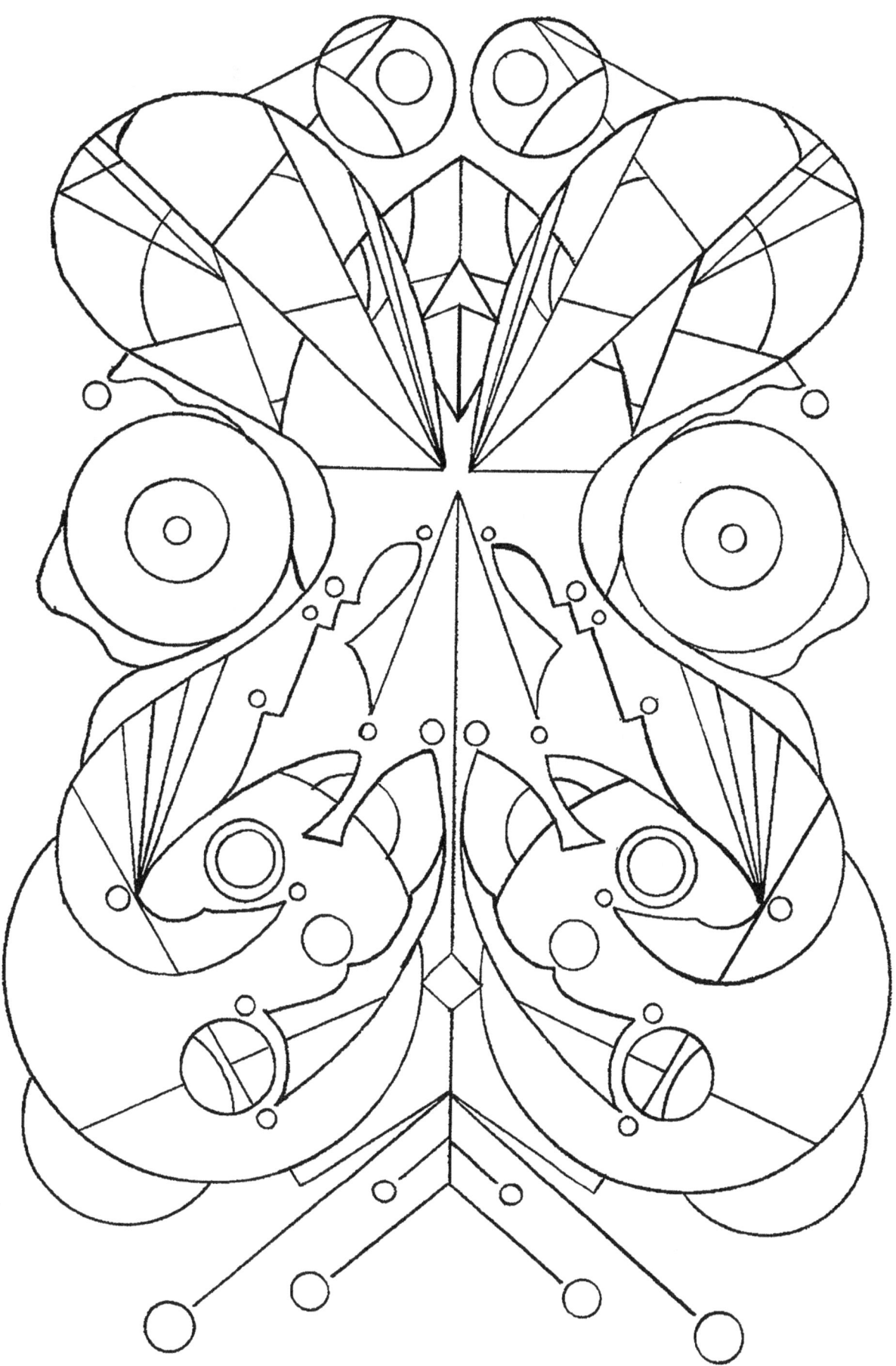

Don't drink and go to meetings.

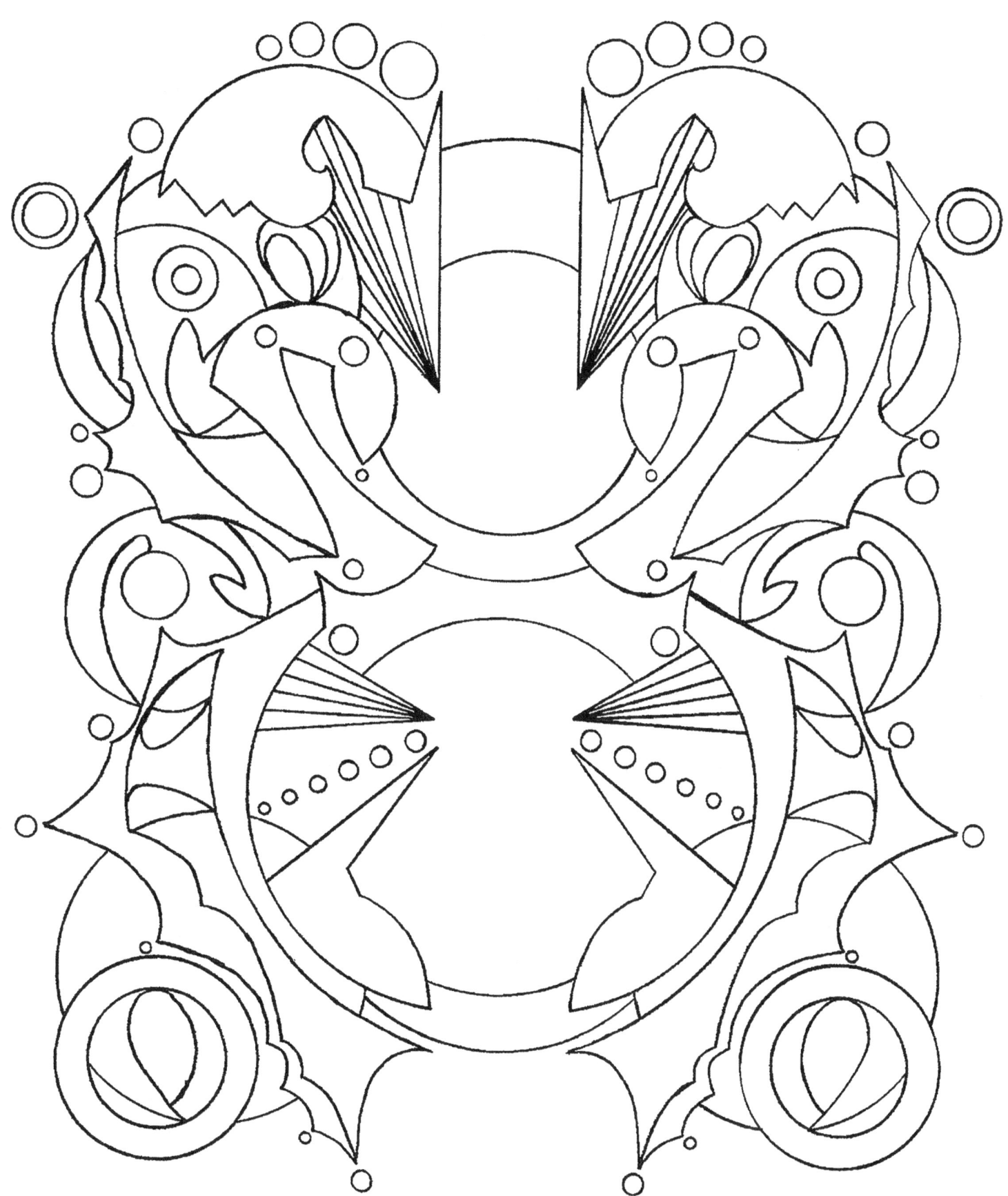

Get a sponsor.

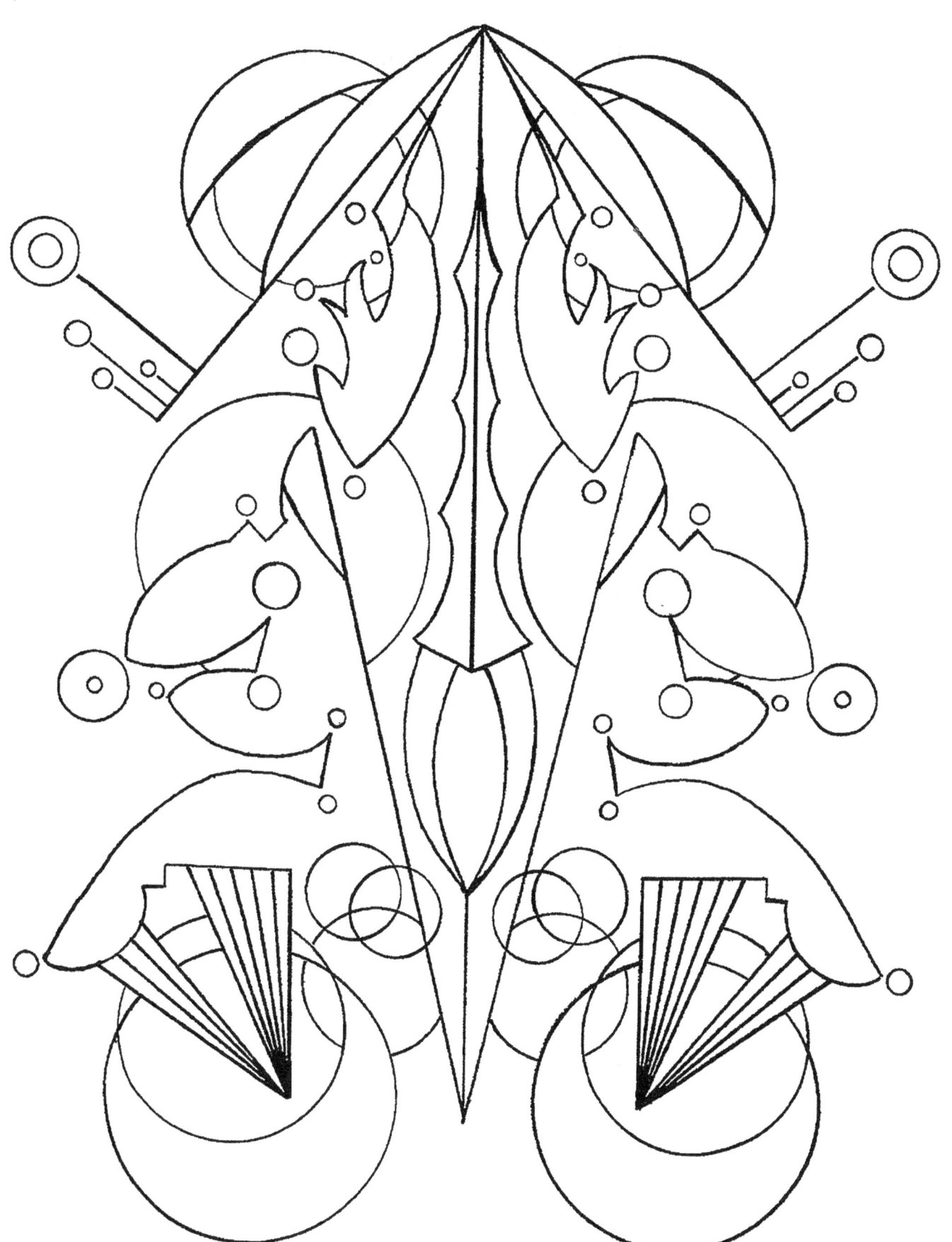

I thank my Higher Power for my sobriety.

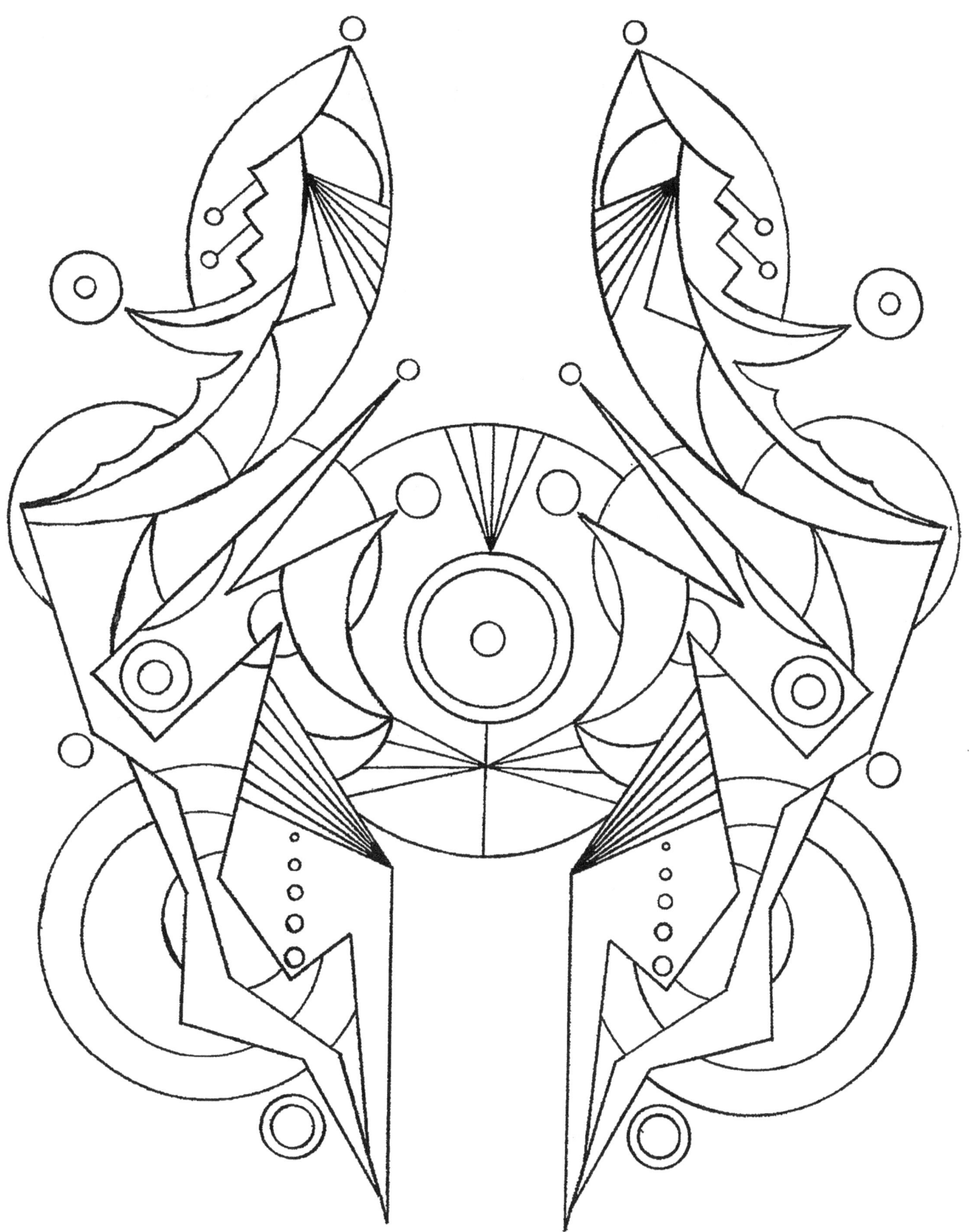

I'm really grateful to be here.

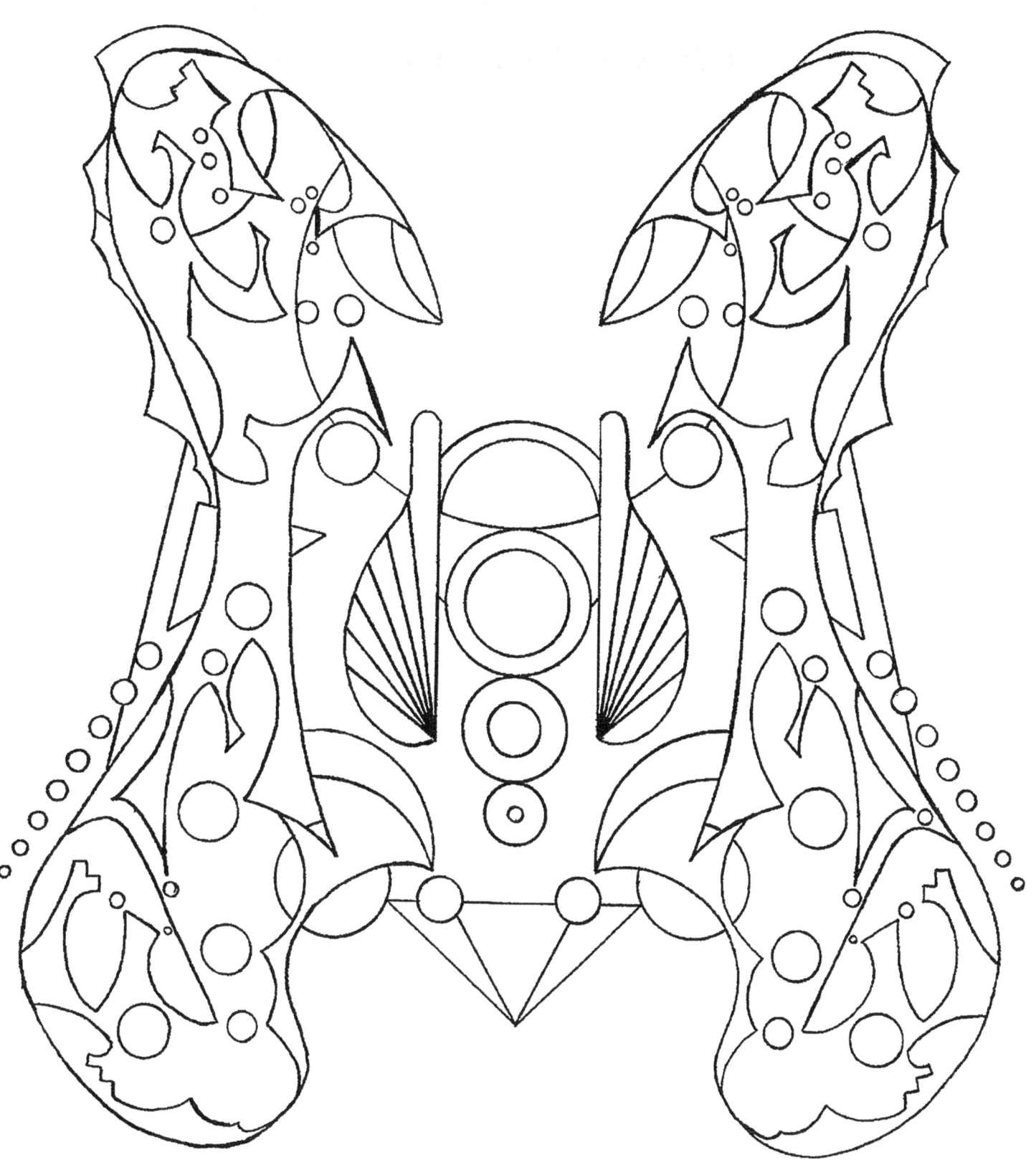

It's always easier to take someone else's inventory.

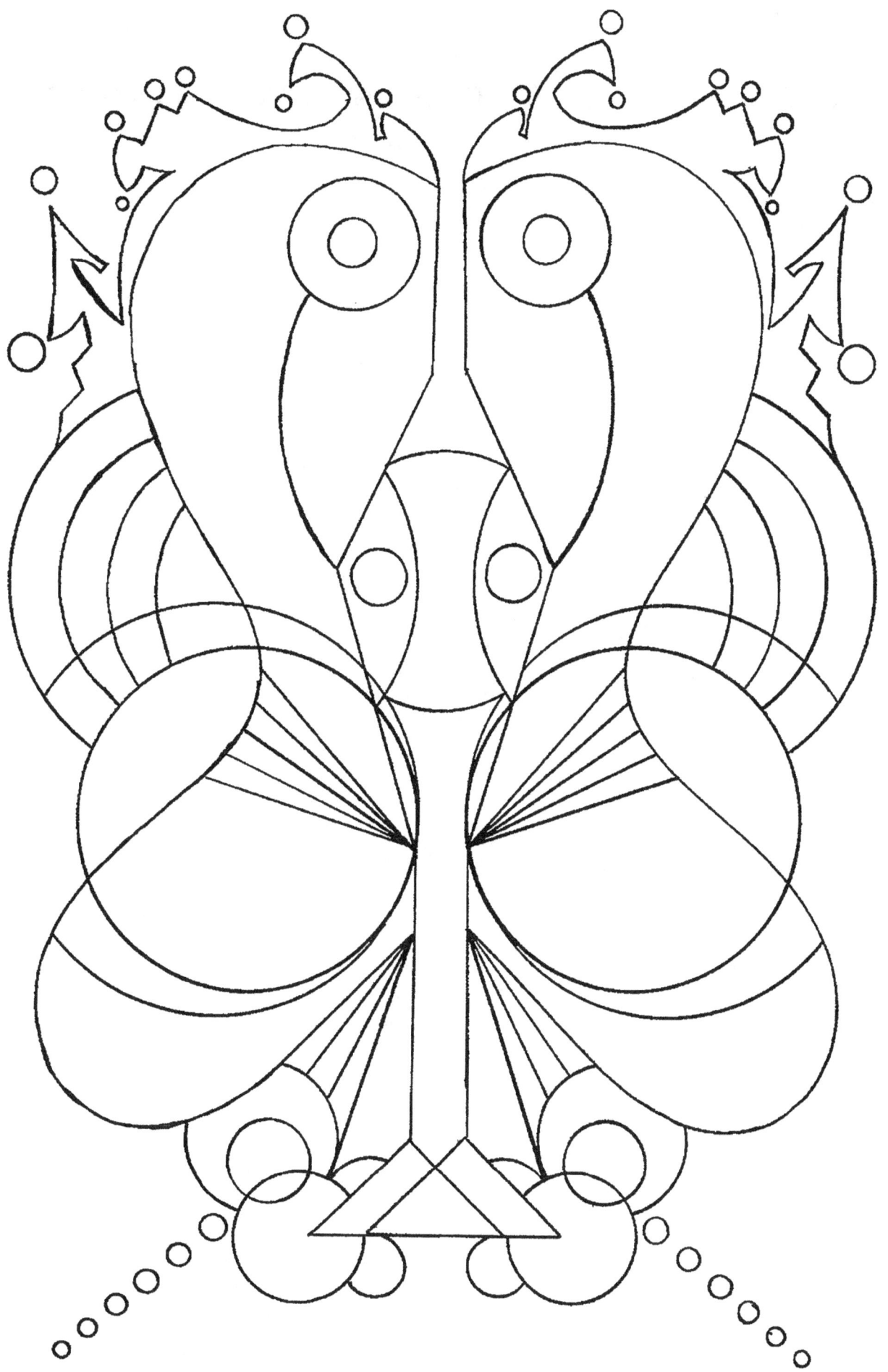

We've got a chair here with your name on it.

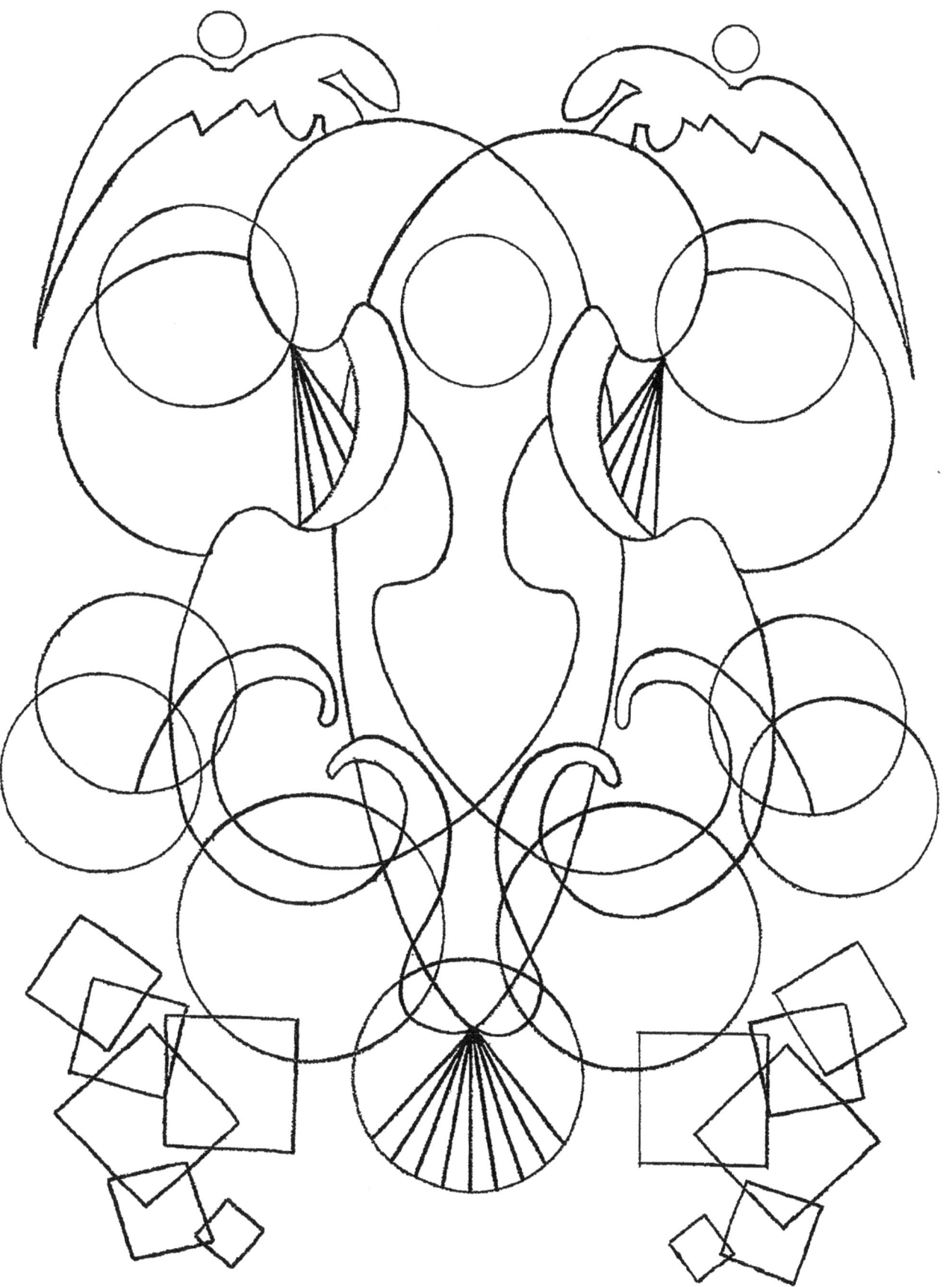

What step are you on?

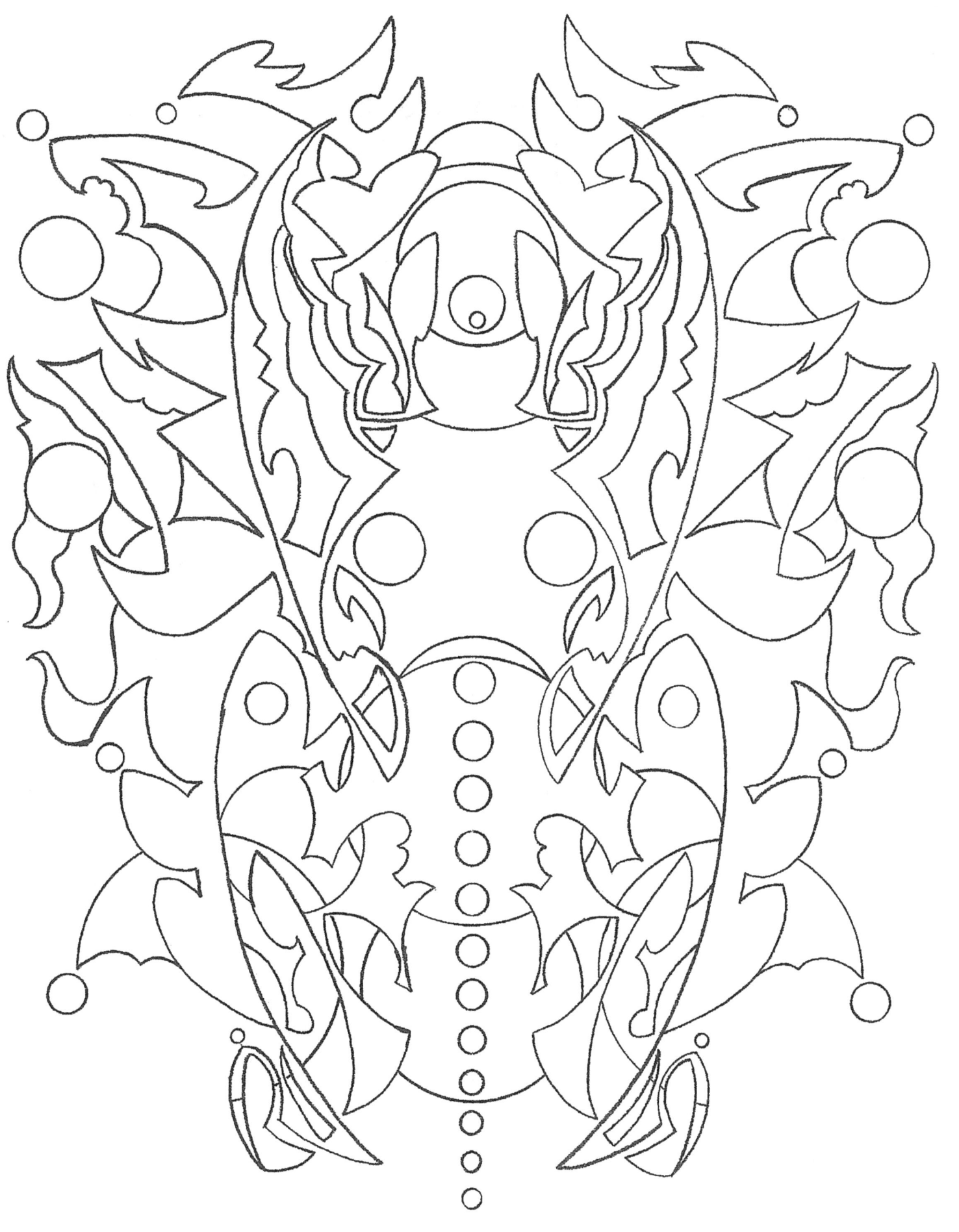

If I don't change, my sobriety date will!

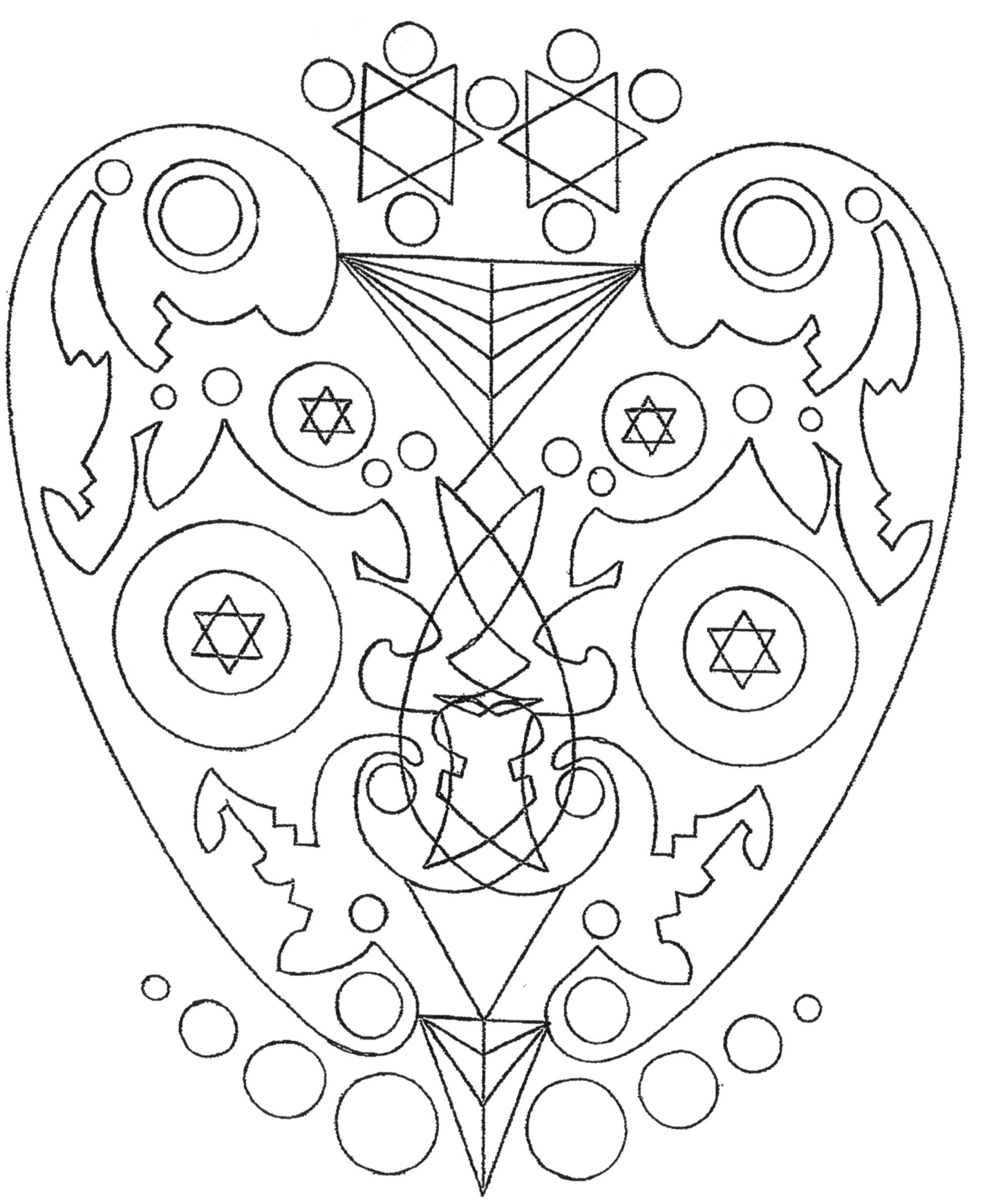

First Things First

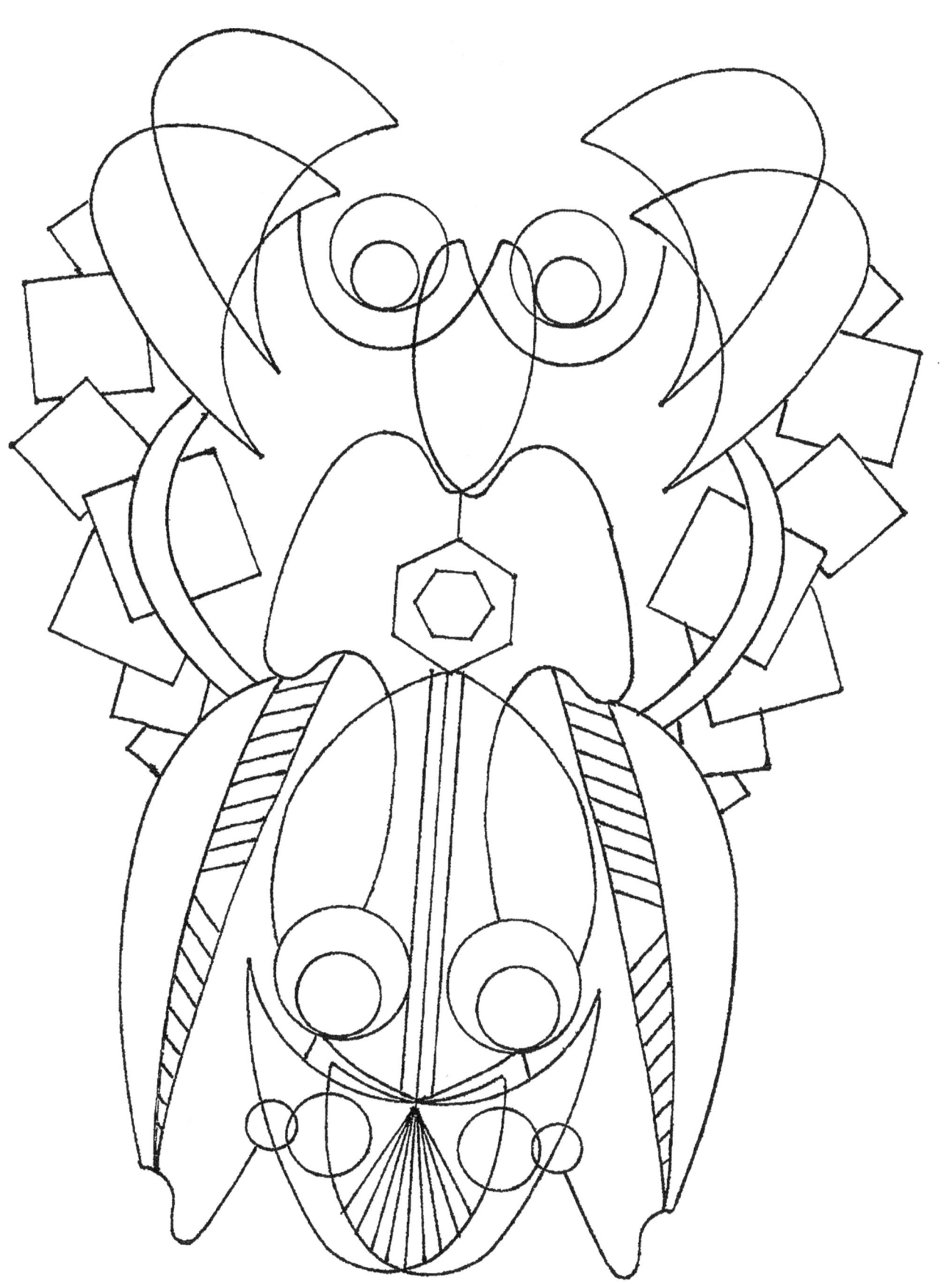

Sit down, shut up and listen.

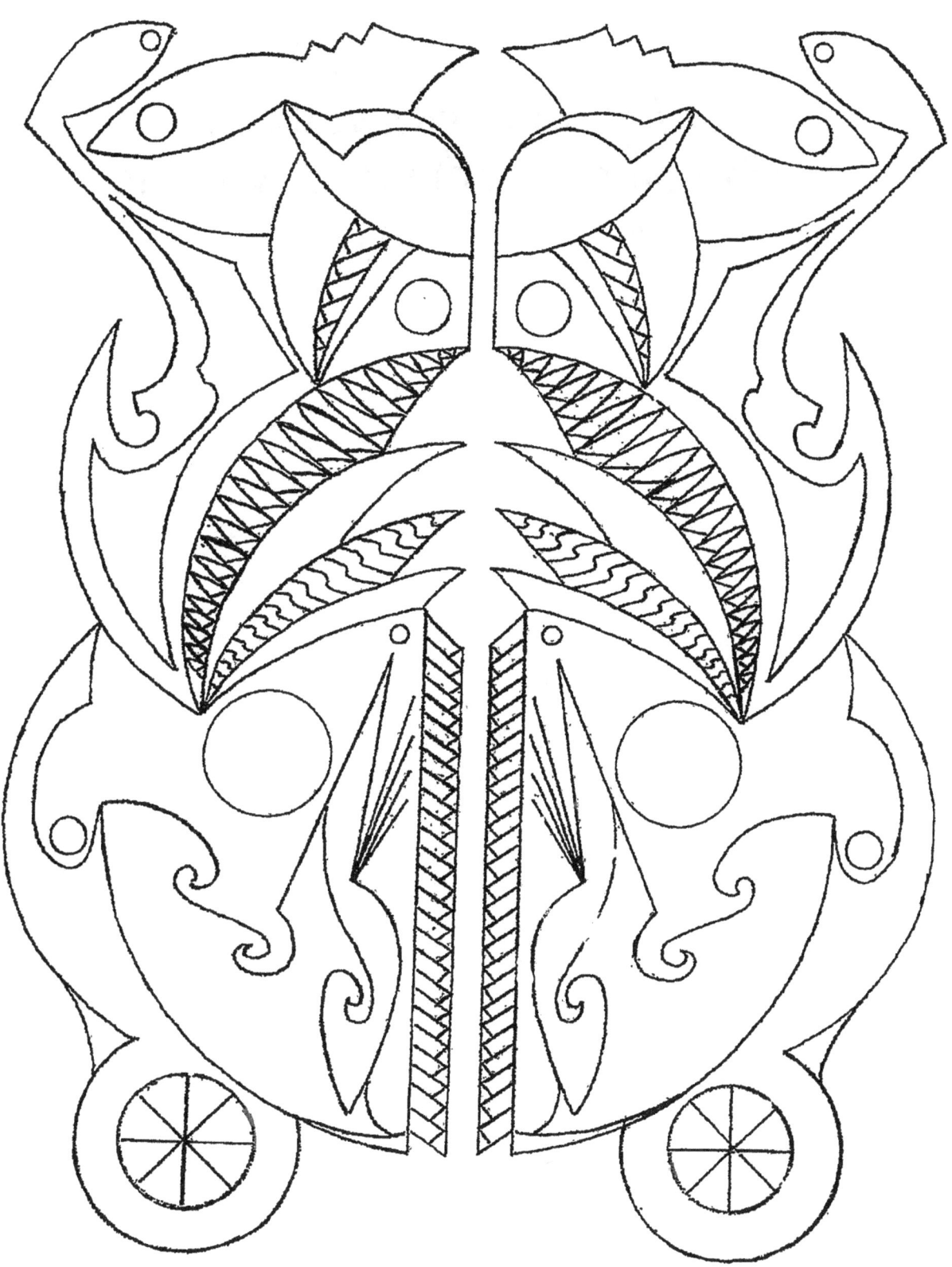

You are 3 people:
Who you think you are.
Who other people think you are.
Who you _really_ are.

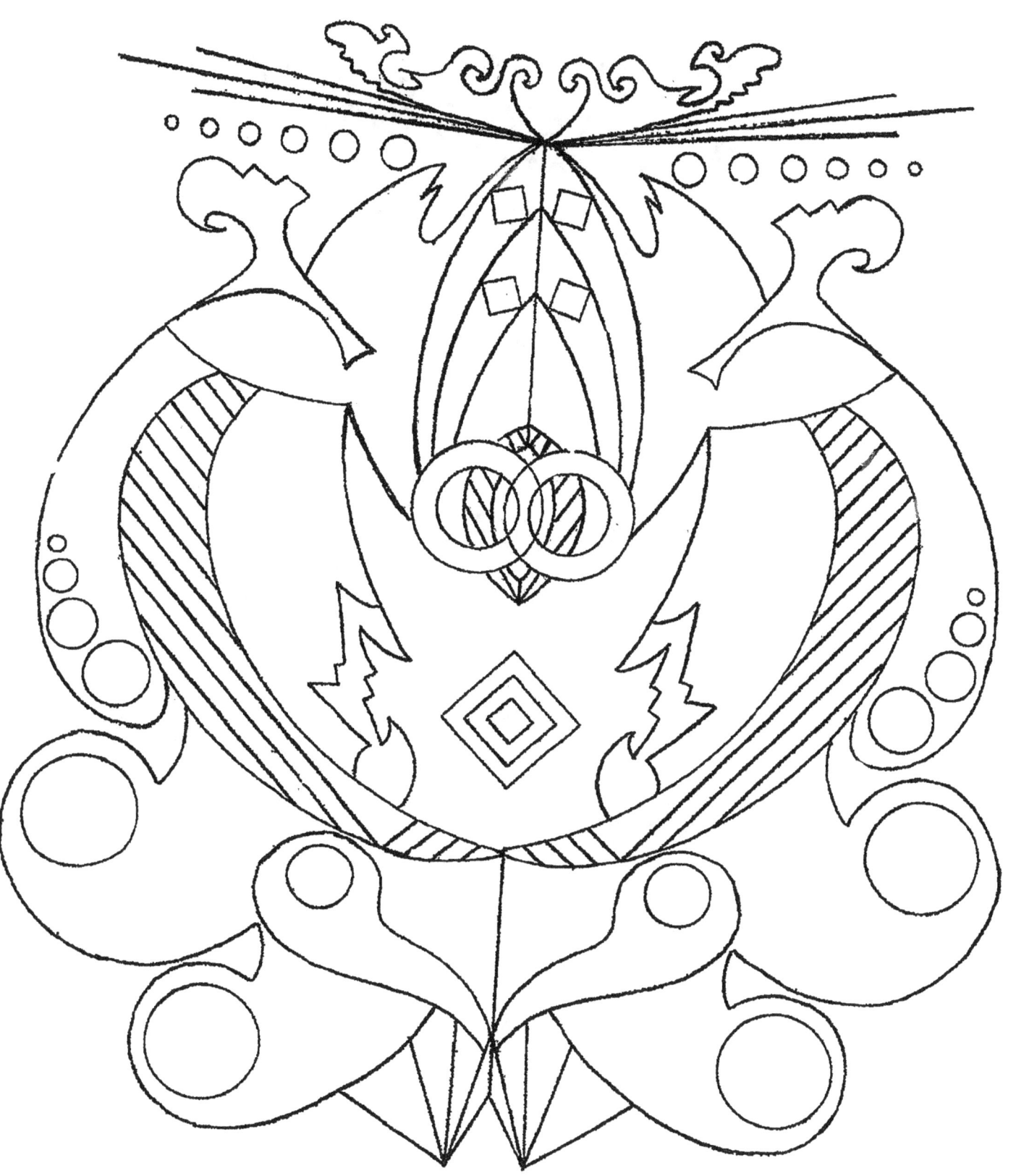

I only have to change one thing -
EVERYTHING!

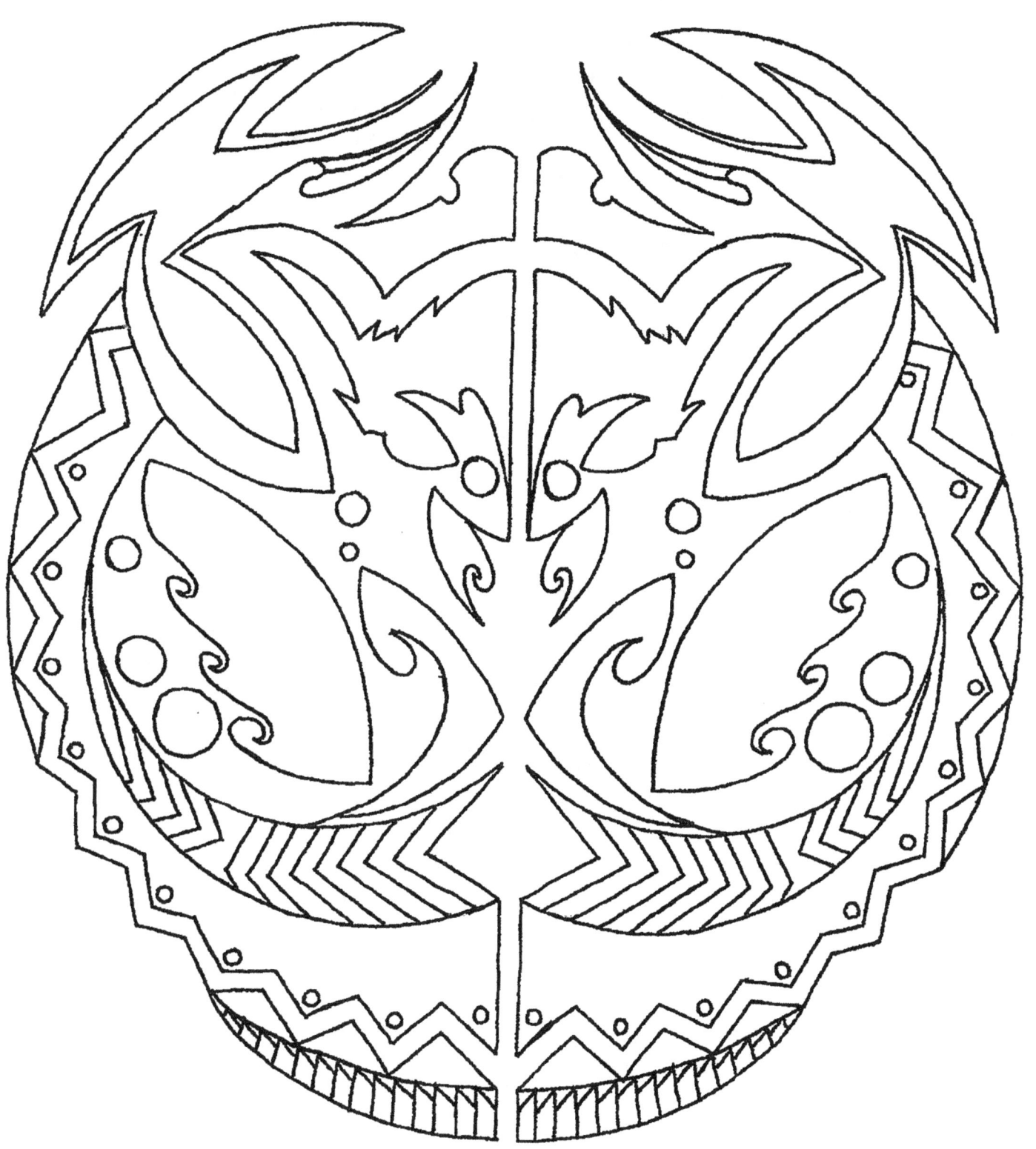

Do I want to be happy or be right?

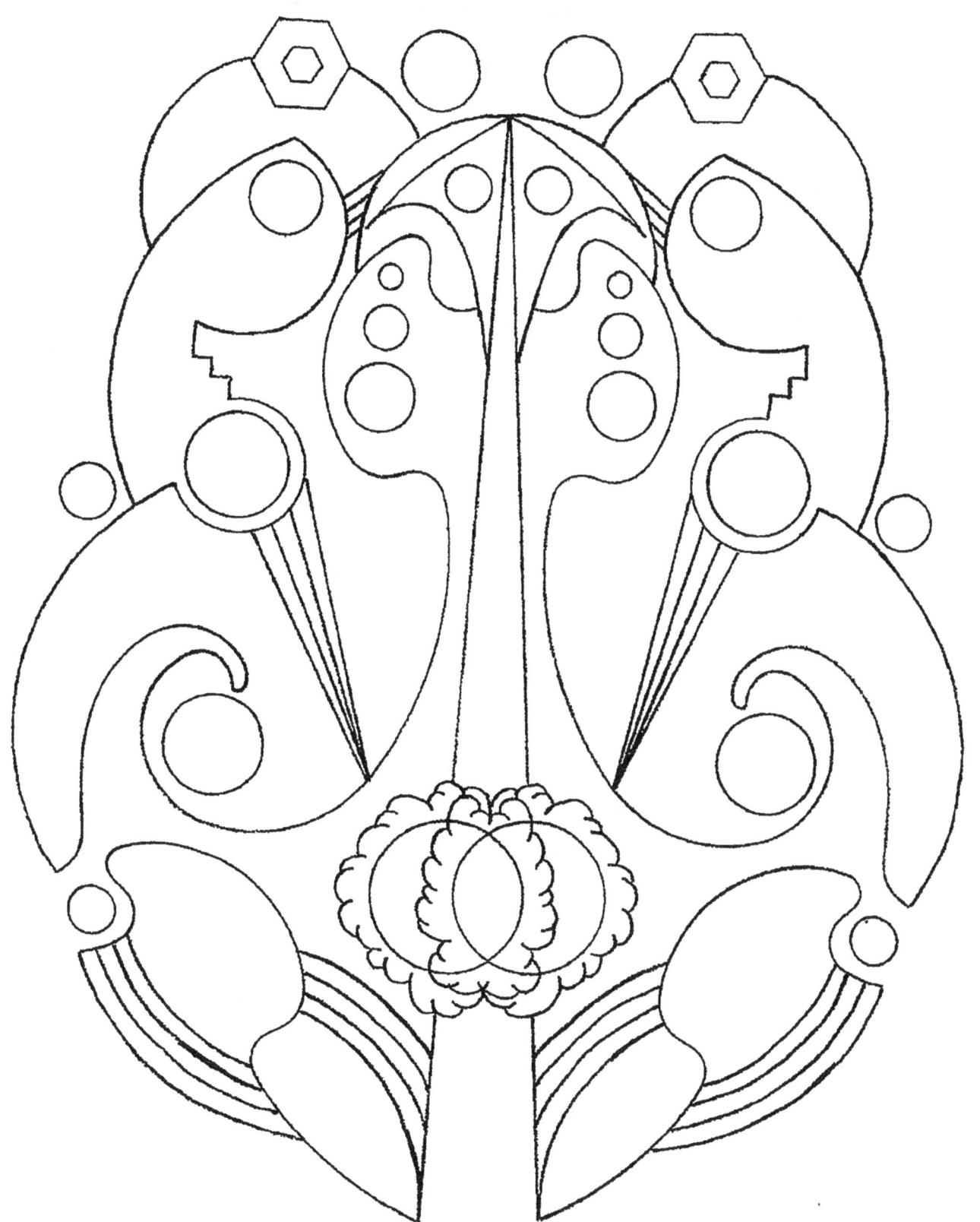

Pain is in the resistance.

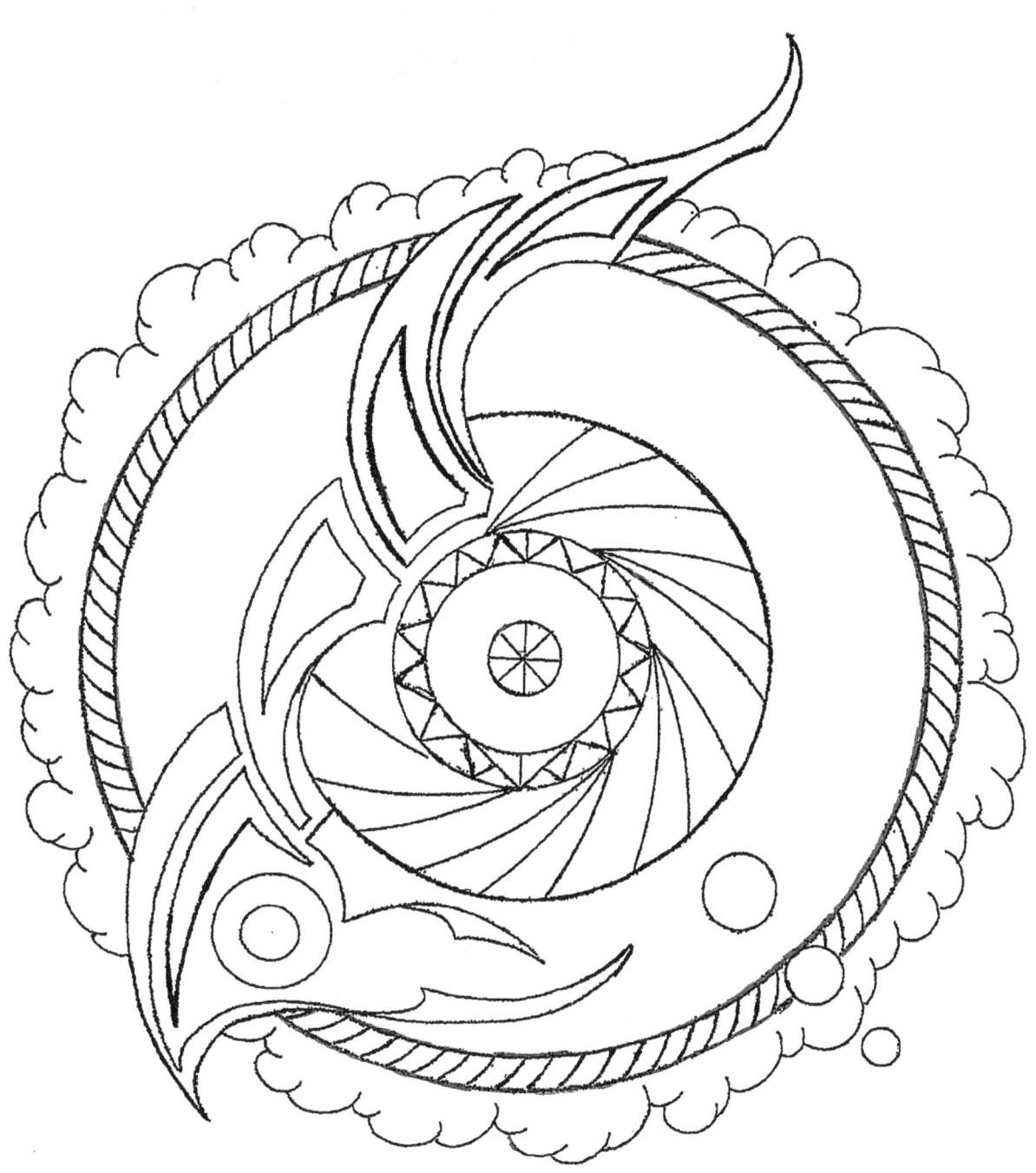

Resentment is a poison I drink to kill the other person.

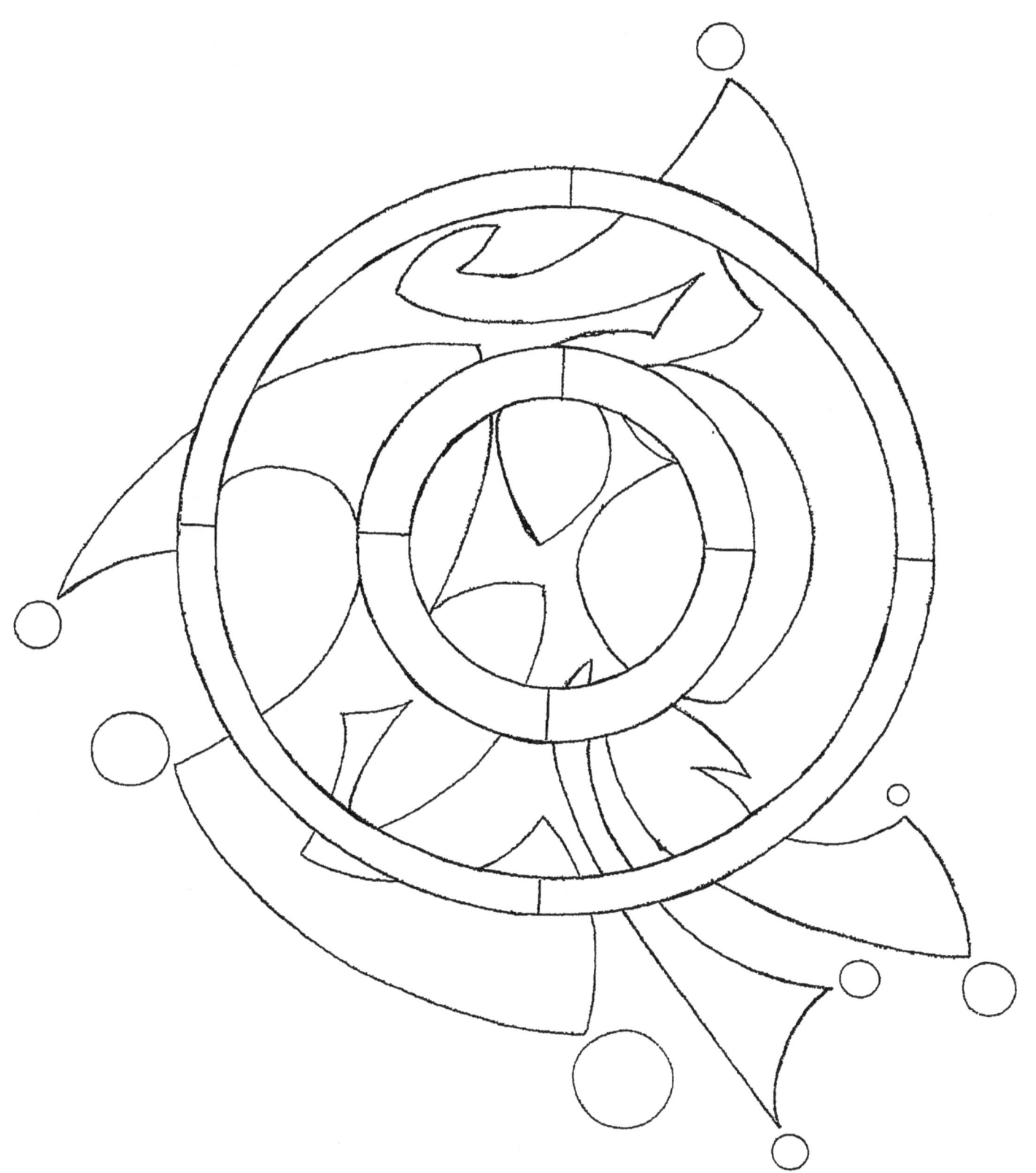

No matter where I go, there I am.

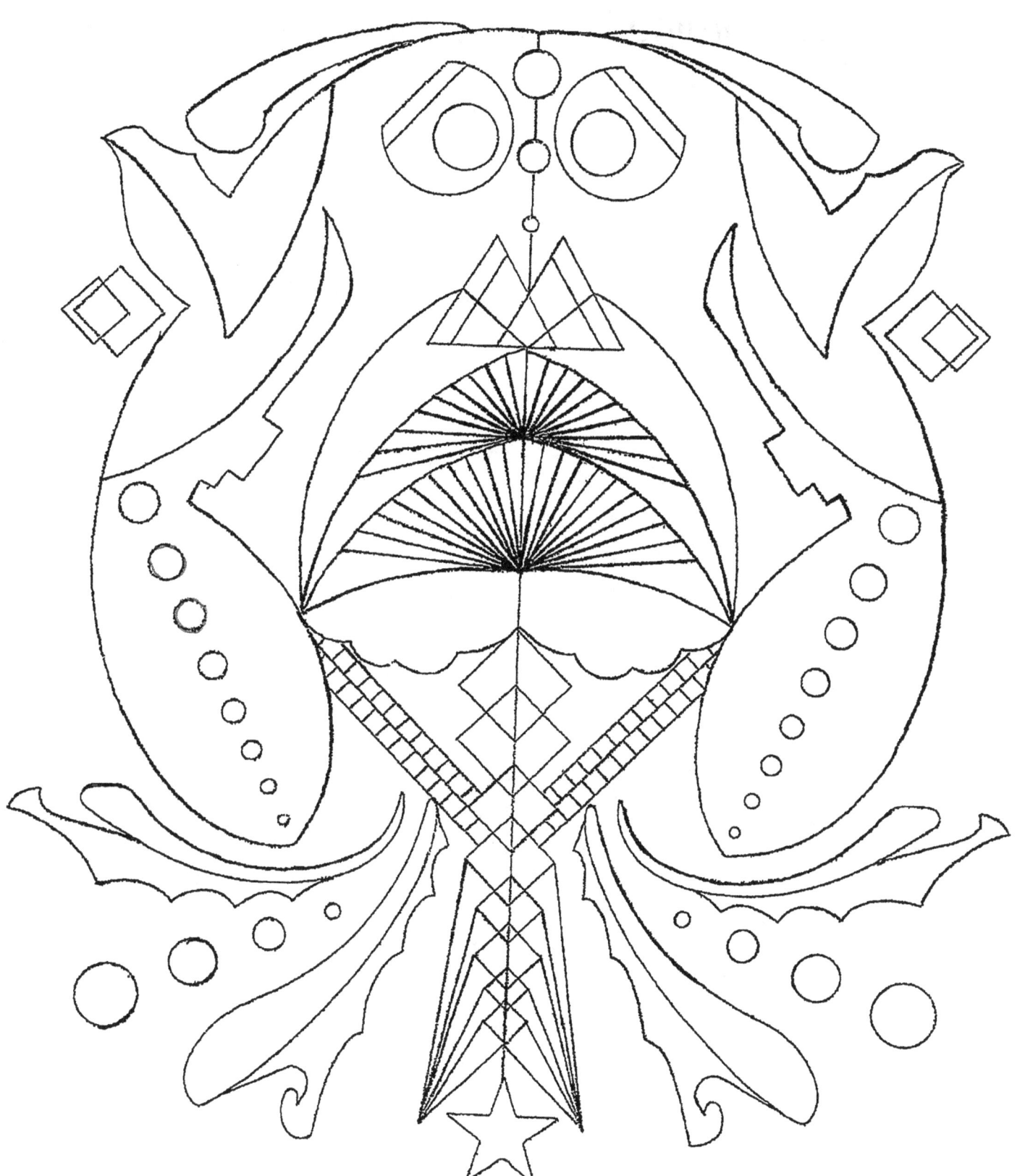

Keep coming back, it works if you work it.